P9-CMT-004

The Tyndale Old Testament Commentaries

General Editor:
PROFESSOR D. J. WISEMAN, O.B.E., M.A., D.Lit., F.B.A.,
F.S.A.

ECCLESIASTES

ECCLESIASTES

AN INTRODUCTION AND COMMENTARY

by

MICHAEL A. EATON, B.D.

Minister, Rouxville Baptist Church, Johannesburg
and Lecturer in Old Testament, The Baptist Theological College
of Southern Africa, Johannesburg

INTER-VARSITY PRESS
LEICESTER, ENGLAND
DOWNERS GROVE, ILLINOIS, U.S.A.

Inter-Varsity Press
38 De Montfort Street, Leicester LE1 7GP, England
Box F, Downers Grove, Illinois 60515 U.S.A.
© *Michael A. Eaton 1983*

First Edition 1983

Inter-Varsity Press, England, is the publishing division of the Universities and Colleges Christian Fellowship (formerly the Inter-Varsity Fellowship), a student movement linking Christian Unions in universities and colleges throughout the British Isles, and a member movement of the International Fellowship of Evangelical Students. For information about local and national activities in Great Britain write to UCCF, 38 De Montfort Street, Leicester LE1 7GP.

InterVarsity Press, U.S.A., is the book-publishing division of Inter-Varsity Christian Fellowship, a student movement active on campus at hundreds of universities, colleges and schools of nursing. For information about local and regional activities, write
IVCF, 233 Langdon St., Madison, WI 53703.

Distributed in Canada through InterVarsity Press, 1875 Leslie St., Unit 10, Don Mills, Ontario M3B 2M5, Canada.

Text set in 10/10 Baskerville

Phototypeset by Nuprint Services Limited, Harpenden, Herts.

Printed

British Library Cataloguing in Publication Data
Eaton, Michael A.
   Ecclesiastes.—(The Tyndale Old Testament commentaries)
   1. Bible. O.T.—Ecclesiastes—Commentaries
   I. Title   II. Series
   223.807   BS1475.3
ISBN 0-85111-637-X (HARDBACK)
ISBN 0-85111-838-0 (PAPERBACK)

Library of Congress Cataloging in Publication Data
Eaton, Michael A., 1942—
   Ecclesiastes: an introduction & commentary.
   (Tyndale Old Testament commentaries; 16)
   Bibliography: p.11
   1. Bible. O.T. Ecclesiastes—Commentaries.
   I. Title.   II. Series
   BS1475.3.E23 1983   223'.807   82-23311
ISBN 0-87784-963-3
ISBN 0-87784-267-1(pbk.)

GENERAL PREFACE

THE aim of this series of *Tyndale Old Testament Commentaries*, as it was in the companion volumes on the New Testament, is to provide the student of the Bible with a handy, up-to-date commentary on each book, with the primary emphasis on exegesis. Major critical questions are discussed in the introductions and additional notes, while undue technicalities have been avoided.

In this series individual authors are, of course, free to make their own distinct contributions and express their own point of view on all debated issues. Within the necessary limits of space they frequently draw attention to interpretations which they themselves do not hold but which represent the stated conclusions of sincere fellow Christians.

In the Old Testament in particular no single English translation is adequate to reflect the original text. The authors of these commentaries freely quote various versions, therefore, or give their own translation, in the endeavour to make the more difficult passages or words meaningful today. Where necessary, words from the Hebrew (and Aramaic) Text underlying their studies are transliterated. This will help the reader who may be unfamiliar with the Semitic languages to identify the word under discussion and thus to follow the argument. It is assumed throughout that the reader will have ready access to one, or more, reliable rendering of the Bible in English.

The book of Ecclesiastes has within it much timeless teaching which is still relevant today. Yet it is a biblical book all too infrequently read and is often quoted or studied only in part. While divergent voices are raised regarding its interpretation and applicability, Mr Eaton seeks to bring a balanced, scholarly view throughout. Nor does he ignore practical references to modern life.

Interest in the meaning and message of the Old Testament

continues undiminished and it is hoped that this series will thus further the systematic study of the revelation of God and his will and ways as seen in these records. It is the prayer of the editor and publisher, as of the authors, that these books will help many to understand, and to respond to, the Word of God today.

D. J. WISEMAN

CONTENTS

AUTHOR'S PREFACE

IF it needs a man who has suffered to write a commentary on Job, and if only a restored rebel can comment on Jonah, perhaps the only person entitled to comment on Ecclesiastes is a cynic who has revolted from the world in disillusionment and disgust. If so, I qualify. It is an experience that many have been through, and from which some never emerge. So it is not surprising to find that a most diverse circle of admirers are drawn to Ecclesiastes with a sense of fellow-feeling for one whom they sense is a 'gentle cynic'. Starting from widely separated perspectives, men have seen life, in W. E. Henley's words, as

> ...a smoke that curls —
> Curls in a flickering skein
> That winds, and whisks and whirls,
> A figment thin and vain,
> Into the great Inane.
> One end for hut and hall!
> One end for cell and stall!
> Burned in one common flame
> Are wisdoms and insanities.
> For this alone we came:
> O vanity of vanities.
>
> *(Of the Nothingness of Things)*

I bear witness that the Preacher's advice, blunt and realistic as it is, is the only remedy to that particular malaise. A 'handful of quietness' (Ec. 4:6) from him who rules the 'times and seasons', Qoheleth's God and mine, is the only cure. I cast this particular piece of bread upon the waters with the prayer that others may make the same discovery.

This small offering owes much to the advice and help of the Rev. J. A. Motyer in the days when he taught at Clifton Theological College and I used to walk from Tyndale Hall to talk about Ecclesiastes. More recently help from Professor D. J. Wiseman of the School of Oriental and African Studies has been much appreciated. Needless to say, the over-all interpretation of Ecclesiastes is my own. I am encouraged that a recent article by R. N. Whybray ('Qoheleth, Preacher of Joy', *Journal for the Study of the Old Testament*, 23, 1982, pp. 87–98) is ready to give much more weight to the joyous side of Ecclesiastes than has been generally the case. It came out too late for me to refer to it in the text.

My thanks go to Mrs Caroline Mullenix who typed the manuscript, and to my wife who prayed the manuscript into existence when I was lost for a spare moment to write. I had the privilege of sharing this material with the morning congregation of Nairobi Baptist Church where I was pastor. The blessings of that particular series of sermons remain with me still.

It is my prayer that God will use this commentary to stimulate fresh thought on Ecclesiastes, that others may be led as I have been through despair to a world-view in which God is God, and people find their rest in him. May a glimpse be caught of the One who fills the gap in Ecclesiastes, our Lord Jesus Christ.

MICHAEL EATON

CHIEF ABBREVIATIONS

Commentaries and Works on Ecclesiastes

Aalders	*Het Boek de Prediker* by G. Ch. Aalders (*Commentar op Het Oude Testament*), 1948.
Barton	*Ecclesiastes* by G. A. Barton (*International Critical Commentary*), 1908.
CPIQ	M. Dahood, 'Canaanite-Phoenician Influence in Qoheleth', *Biblica*, 33, 1952, pp. 30-52, 191-221.
Delitzsch	*The Song of Songs and Ecclesiastes* by F. Delitzsch, 1891.
Ellermeier	*Qohelet I/1, Untersuchengen zum Buche Qohelet* by F. Ellermeier, 1967.
Galling	*Die Fünf Megilloth* by K. Galling, 1940, ²1969.
Ginsberg	*Supplementary Studies in Koheleth* by H. L. Ginsberg, 1952.
Ginsburg	*Coheleth* by C. D. Ginsburg, 1861.
Gordis	*Koheleth – the Man and His World* by R. Gordis, 1955.
Graetz	*Kohelet oder der Salomonische Prediger* by H. Graetz, 1871.
Hengstenberg	*Commentary on Ecclesiastes* by E. W. Hengstenberg, 1869.
Hertzberg	*Der Prediger, Das Buch Esther* by H. W. Hertzberg and H. Bardtke (*Kommentar zum Alten Testament*), 1963.
Jastrow	*A Gentle Cynic* by M. Jastrow, 1919.
Jones	*Proverbs, Ecclesiastes* by E. Jones (*Torch Bible Commentaries*), 1961.
Kidner	*A Time to Mourn, and a Time to Dance* by D. Kidner (*The Bible speaks today*), 1976.
Lauha	*Kohelet* by A. Lauha (*Biblischer Kommentar Altes Testament*), 1978.

CHIEF ABBREVIATIONS

Leupold	*Exposition of Ecclesiastes* by H. C. Leupold, 1952.
Luther	'Notes on Ecclesiastes', *Luther's Works*, vol. 15, 1972.
Lys	*L'Ecclésiaste ou que vaut la vie?* by D. Lys, vol. 1, 1977.
McNeile	*An Introduction to Ecclesiastes* by A. H. McNeile, 1904.
PBQ	M. Dahood, 'The Phoenician Background of Qoheleth', *Biblica*, 47, 1966, pp. 264-282.
Plumptre	*Ecclesiastes or The Preacher* by E. H. Plumptre, 1881.
Podechard	*L'Ecclésiaste* by E. Podechard, 1912.
Power	*Ecclesiastes or The Preacher* by A. D. Power, 1952.
QRD	M. Dahood, 'Qoheleth and Recent Discoveries', *Biblica*, 39, 1958, pp. 302-318.
Ranston	*Ecclesiastes and the Early Greek Wisdom Literature* by H. Ranston, 1925.
Rylaarsdam	*Proverbs, Ecclesiastes, Song of Solomon* by J. C. Rylaarsdam, 1965.
Scott	*Proverbs, Ecclesiastes* by R. B. Y. Scott (*Anchor Bible*), 1965.
Thilo	*Der Prediger* by M. Thilo, 1923.
Wardlaw	*Lectures on the Book of Ecclesiastes* by R. Wardlaw, 2 vols., 1838.
Wildeboer	*Der Prediger* by G. Wildeboer, 1898.
Williams	*Ecclesiastes* by A. L. Williams (*The Cambridge Bible*), 1922.
Wright	*The Book of Koheleth* by C. H. H. Wright, 1883.
Zimmerli	*Das Buch Des Predigers Salomo* by W. Zimmerli, 1962.

Bible Translations and Versions

AV	Authorized Verson (King James), 1611.
ASV	American Standard Version, 1901.
Berkeley	Revised Berkeley Version, 1974.
GNB	Good News Bible, 1976.
Heb.	Hebrew.
JB	Jerusalem Bible, 1966.
LXX	The Septuagint (Greek Version of the Old Testament).
mg.	margin.

Moffatt	*A New Translation of the Bible* by J. Moffatt, 1935.
MT	Massoretic Text.
NAB	The New American Bible, 1970.
NASV	New American Standard Version, 1971.
NEB	The New English Bible, 1970.
NIV	New International Version, 1978.
Peshitta	*The Old Testament in Syriac* (E. J. Brill, Leiden), part II, fasc. 5, 1979.
RSV	Revised Standard Version, 1952.
RV	Revised Version, 1885.
Targum	A. Sperber, *The Bible in Aramaic*, vol. IVA, 1968.

Other Reference Works

ANET	*Ancient Near Eastern Texts* edited by J. B. Pritchard, [3]1969.
BDB	*Hebrew-English Lexicon of the Old Testament* by F. Brown, S. R. Driver and C. A. Briggs, 1907.
DS	*Hebrew Syntax* by A. B. Davidson, [3]1901.
DTTML	*Dictionary of the Targumim, Talmud Babli, Yerushalmi and Midrashic Literature* by M. Jastrow, 1971 edition.
GK	*Hebrew Grammar* by W. Gesenius, E. Kautzsch and A. E. Cowley, [2]1910.
IB	*The Interpreter's Bible* edited by G. A. Buttrick *et al.*, 12 vols., 1952-57.
IBD	*The Illustrated Bible Dictionary* edited by N. Hillyer *et al.*, 3 vols., 1980.
IDB	*The Interpreter's Dictionary of the Bible* edited by G. A. Buttrick *et al.*, 4 vols., 1962.
Joüon	*Grammaire de l'Hébreu Biblique* by P. Joüon, 1923.
Lambert	*Babylonian Wisdom Literature* by W. G. Lambert, 1960.
Leiman	*The Canonisation of the Hebrew Scriptures* by S. Z. Leiman, 1976.
LS	*A Greek-English Lexicon* by H. Liddell and R. Scott, [9]1940.
NBCR	*The New Bible Commentary Revised* edited by D. Guthrie *et al.*, 1970.
SIAIW	*Studies in Ancient Israelite Wisdom* edited by J. L Crenshaw, 1976.

CHIEF ABBREVIATIONS

TDNT	*Theological Dictionary of the New Testament* edited by G. Kittel and G. Friedrich; E.T. edited by G. W. Bromiley, 10 vols., 1964-76.
UBD	*Unger's Bible Dictionary* by M. F. Unger, 1957.
WIANE	*Wisdom in Israel and in the Ancient Near East* edited by M. Noth and D. W. Thomas, 1955.

References to Ibn Ezra and Kimchi (Jewish commentators) and Aquila (a translator into Greek) are dependent on secondary sources.

Journals

ASTI	*Annual of the Swedish Theological Institute.*
BASOR	*Bulletin of the American Schools of Oriental Research.*
Bib	*Biblica.*
CBQ	*Catholic Bible Quarterly.*
EQ	*Evangelical Quarterly.*
HUCA	*Hebrew Union College Annual.*
IEJ	*Israel Exploration Journal.*
JAOS	*Journal of the American Oriental Society.*
JBL	*Journal of Biblical Literature.*
JEA	*Journal of Egyptian Archaeology.*
JNES	*Journal of Near Eastern Studies.*
JNSL	*Journal of Northwest Semitic Languages.*
JQR	*Jewish Quarterly Review.*
JSS	*Journal of Semitic Studies.*
JTS	*Journal of Theological Studies.*
OTS	*Oudtestamentische Studiën.*
PEQ	*Palestine Exploration Quarterly.*
SJT	*Scottish Journal of Theology.*
TB	*Tyndale Bulletin.*
VT	*Vetus Testamentum.*
VTS	*Supplement to Vetus Testamentum.*
WTJ	*Westminster Theological Journal.*
ZATW	*Zeitschrift für die alttestamentliche Wissenschaft.*

INTRODUCTION

I. THE TEXT OF ECCLESIASTES

THE primary source of the text of Ecclesiastes, as of any other Old Testament book, is a text-form established in or near the first century AD, vocalized and annotated by Massoretes ('transmitters') *c.* AD 500–1000, known as the Massoretic text. This was originally written in a consonantal form, but from the sixth century onwards several systems of vocalization arose. In the ninth and tenth centuries one of these, the Tiberian system, became the standard and is still used by Old Testament scholars. The text printed in *Biblica Hebraica Stuttgartensia* (1970) is that of a manuscript dated AD 1008, a copy of a text produced by the Tiberian textual scholar Ben Asher in the tenth century. Any student of the Old Testament must start from the Massoretic text but, because of inevitable copyists' errors, must take into account other Hebrew texts that may be known and ancient translations which had access to earlier texts.[1]

In the case of Ecclesiastes we are fortunate to have four pieces of manuscript discovered at Qumran and published in 1954,[2] containing fragments of chs 5 – 7. On the basis of style of script these have been dated in the mid-second century BC. Most of the variations are purely orthographic. In addition Muilenburg lists ten places where the Qumran text differs from the Massoretic text. The Qumran text (4Q Ec) reads 'for' instead of 'as' at 5:14, omits 'and' at 5:15 and 7:6, reverses the order of two words in 6:3, has 'house of pleasure' instead of 'house of drinking' at 7:2, has 'corrupt' instead of 'destroy' in 7:7, 'help' instead of 'strengthen' in 7:19, and slight variations with virtually no change of meaning

---

[1] For fuller details, *cf.* B. J. Roberts, *The Old Testament and Versions* (1951); E. Würthwein, *The Text of the Old Testament* (1957); R. K. Harrison, *Introduction to the Old Testament* (1970), pp. 211–243.

[2] *Cf.* J. Muilenburg, 'A Qoheleth Scroll From Qumran', *BASOR*, 135, 1954, pp. 20–28.

in 6:4, 6; 7:4.[1] None of this amounts to very much, and the manuscript tends generally to confirm the reliability of the Massoretic tradition.

Another source of textual evidence is provided by the ancient translations of the Old Testament. The most important of these is the Greek Septuagint (LXX), probably translated in stages beginning with the Pentateuch in the third century and substantially completed by the late second century BC. It is uncertain at what date Ecclesiastes was translated. O. Eissfeldt claims that Ben Sira had all of the law, the prophets and the writings before him in Greek *c.* 130 BC,[2] whereas D. Barthélemy claims that the LXX Ecclesiastes is in fact the work of Aquila, who produced a rival Greek translation in the second century AD.[3] The LXX translation is quite literal and generally bears witness to the Massoretic tradition.

The Syriac version, known as the Peshitta, was made in the early or middle second century AD.[4]

Another witness is Jerome's fourth-century Vulgate, a revision of an earlier Latin version. Although the Vulgate is a translation of the Hebrew text in the Massoretic tradition, Jerome's textual decisions were also influenced by the LXX.[5]

The Ethiopic text of Ecclesiastes, dated by S. A. B. Mercer some time before AD 650, reveals an acquaintance with the Massoretic tradition, the Vulgate, and perhaps the Old Latin and Syriac. Mercer points to eighteen instances where it follows the Massoretic text against the LXX and to fourteen instances where it shows knowledge of a pre-Massoretic Hebrew text.[6]

[1] The variations are:

	4Q Ec	MT
5:14	*ky*ʾ	*k'šr*
5:15	*gm*	*wgm*
6:3	*hnpl mmnw*	*mmnw hnpl*
6:4	*hlk*	*ylk*
6:6	*w'm lw'*	*w'lw*
7:2	*š]mḥh*	*mšth*
7:4	*byt*	*bbyt*
7:6	*gm*	*wgm*
7:7	*wyʿwh*	*wy'bd*
7:19	*tʿzr*	*tʿz*

[2] O. Eissfeldt, *The Old Testament – An Introduction* (1965), p. 703.
[3] D. Barthélemy, *Les devanciers d'Aquila* (*VTS*, 10, 1963), pp. 32f., 158f.
[4] *The Old Testament in Syriac*, part II, fasc. 5 (Leiden, 1979).
[5] *Cf. Biblia Sacra iuxta Latinam Vulgatam Versionem*, XI, *Proverbia, Ecclesiastes, Canticum Canticorum* (1957).
[6] *Cf.* S. A. B. Mercer, *The Ethiopic Text of the Book of Ecclesiastes; The Oriental Research Series*, 6 (1931).

The Aramaic Targum to Ecclesiastes is of little significance for textual study. It is a free paraphrase not earlier than the fifth century AD, and is of interest primarily as one stage in the history of interpretation.[1]

The study of these versions leads one to the conclusion that the text of Ecclesiastes is well preserved and has fewer difficulties than many Old Testament books. The Qumran texts and the various versions generally support the Massoretic tradition.

II. THE DATE, AUTHORSHIP AND LITERARY PROVENANCE OF ECCLESIASTES

Life in this world does not fundamentally change, and we do not need a date for Ecclesiastes in order to receive its message. It is part of the genius of the Preacher's thought that it stands on its own feet at any time and in any place. The book in fact provides meagre clues to its date: language, possible dependence on foreign thought, and internal claims.

Language

The mid-twentieth century has seen the rise of a three-sided debate concerning the linguistic background of Ecclesiastes. After a tentative suggestion by D. S. Margoliouth that its language is 'not so much late Hebrew as foreign Hebrew',[2] amplified by F. C. Burkitt in 1921,[3] F. Zimmermann formally proposed in 1945 that Ecclesiastes is a translation from an Aramaic original.[4] This was supported by C. C. Torrey in 1948[5] and by H. L. Ginsberg in 1950.[6] These suggestions led to a series of replies by R. Gordis, who maintained that the Hebrew of Ecclesiastes is authentic but late.[7] The discussion further developed in 1952 when M. Dahood suggested that Ecclesiastes was written in Phoenician

---

[1] *Cf.* A. Sperber, *The Bible in Aramaic*, vol. IVA, *The Hagiographa* (1968).

[2] *The Jewish Encyclopaedia* ([3]1923), 5, p. 33.

[3] F. C. Burkitt, 'Is Ecclesiastes a Translation?', *JTS*, 23, 1921, pp. 23–26.

[4] F. Zimmermann, 'The Aramaic Provenance of Qohelet', *JQR*, 36, 1945–6, pp. 17–45; followed by 'The Question of Hebrew in Qohelet', *JQR*, 40, 1949, pp. 79–102.

[5] C. C. Torrey, 'The Question of the Original Language of Qohelet', *JQR*, 39, 1948, pp. 151–160.

[6] H. L. Ginsberg, *Studies in Koheleth* (1950).

[7] R. Gordis, 'The Original Language of Qoheleth', *JQR*, 37, 1946, pp. 67–84; 'The Translation Theory of Qoheleth Re-Examined', *JQR*, 40, 1949, pp. 103–116; 'Koheleth – Hebrew or Aramaic?', *JBL*, 71, 1952, pp. 93–109.

ECCLESIASTES

orthography and shows signs of Canaanite-Phoenician literary influence.[1] Again R. Gordis replied rebutting Dahood's theory.[2]

The Aramaisms of Ecclesiastes are not necessarily proof of a late date. True, there are Aramaisms in the book,[3] indeed, their proportion is quite high, but since the quantity of material is so small one must be cautious in attributing too much significance to them. They may be expected in biblical Hebrew from the tenth century BC, increasing as the centuries go by, culminating in the sixth to fourth centuries BC. They are of comparatively little significance for dating.[4]

Even less is it likely that an Aramaic original underlies Ecclesiastes. To review the many intricate arguments involved is beyond the scope of the present work; but it must be said that the suggestions of Zimmermann, Torrey and Ginsberg are upheld only by a large number of tortuous emendations and suggested mistranslations, exhibiting considerable ingenuity of thought but carrying very little conviction. One small indication that the theory is suspect is the combination of the verbs *mkk* and *dlp* in 10:18. The two verbs in combination are an old Canaanite cliché.[5] That it should be the result of a translation from Aramaic seems unlikely.

[1] M. Dahood, 'Canaanite-Phoenician Influence in Qoheleth', *Bib*, 33, 1952, pp. 30–52, 191–221; 'Qoheleth and Recent Discoveries', *Bib*, 39, 1958, pp. 302–318. Similar suggestions had been made earlier by C. H. Gordon, *Ugaritic Literature* (1947), p. 123.

[2] R. Gordis, 'Was Koheleth a Phoenician?', *JBL*, 74, 1955, pp. 103–114; 'Qoheleth and Qumran – A Study in Style', *Bib*, 41, 1960, pp. 395–410.

[3] The number of Aramaisms is a matter of dispute. A possible list is: *kᵉbār* (1:10, *etc.*), *mᵉdînâ* (2:8; 5:7), *šabbēᵃḥ* (4:2; *cf.* 8:15), *'inyan* (1:13, *etc.*), *tāqan* (1:15; *cf.* 7:13; 12:9), *tāqap* (4:12; 6:10), *'al-diḇrat* (3:18; 7:14; 8:12), *pēšer* (8:1), *šilṭon* (8:4), *dᵉrāḇ* (9:18), *gûmmāṣ* (10:8), *yissāḵen* (10:9), *ben-ḥôrîm* (10:17), *maddā'* (10:20), *bāṭᵉlû* (12:3), and the vocalization of *'ᵃbadêhem* (9:1) and *kᵉḇēl* (1:2, *etc.*). *Cf.* O. Loretz, *Qohelet und der Alte Orient* (1964), pp. 24–25; *cf.* also M. Wagner, *Die Lexicalischen und Grammatikalischen Aramäismen im Alttestamentlichen Hebräisch* (1966), who maintains that 3.1 per cent of Ecclesiastes is Aramaic in origin (p. 145). A similar view is held by C. F. Whitley (*Koheleth* (1979), pp. 147f.), who dates the book within 152–145 BC. Older lists (*e.g.* those by F. Delitzsch and C. H. H. Wright) need revision in the light of fuller knowledge of Semitic languages.

[4] A. Hurvitz, 'The Chronological Significance of "Aramaisms" in Biblical Hebrew', *IEJ*, 18, 1968, pp. 234–240, deals with the difficulties of the subject and the circumstances under which Aramaisms may be significant. Judged by his criteria the Preacher's use of *sālaṭ* (perhaps replacing the earlier *māšal*) may be evidence of late date (but see p. 20, footnote 4). However, one word cannot be of that much weight.

[5] *Cf.* C. H. Gordon, *Ugaritic Textbook* (1963), p. 180, text 68:17.

The question of Canaanite-Phoenician influence is more difficult to handle. Dahood argues that at one stage the text of Ecclesiastes had considerably less *matres lectiones* (consonants used as vowels to aid reading) than in the Massoretic text. Nouns with a feminine ending in *–t*, a conditional particle *'lw*, the particle *s–*, the erratic use of the article, the infinitive absolute followed by an independent pronoun, the independent use of the pronoun to express the verb 'to be', the use of *'ādām*, the phrase *under the sun, the seven…eight* phrasing (Ec. 11:2), all have Phoenician and Canaanite parallels but within the Old Testament are distinctive of Ecclesiastes. But it is doubtful if even the cumulative weight of all the parallels to be found point to an original in 'Phoenician orthography'. The work of the 'Dahood school' has itself suggested that a considerable quantity of Ugaritic and Phoenician parallels can be found to sections of the Old Testament. Job, Psalms, Proverbs, Isaiah, Ezekiel and Nahum are among books explored along these lines.

The difficulty is that the linguistic data show that Ecclesiastes does not fit into any known section of the history of the Hebrew language. It is dissimilar to works which claim to be Solomonic (Song of Songs; parts of Proverbs); it does not correspond to the fourth-century Hebrew of Malachi or Ezra; it does not tally with the Hebrew of the Qumran scrolls. Two words, *pardēs* and *pitgam*, are often thought to be Persian loanwords. This may be so; in which case our present Ecclesiastes was written or edited[1] in or after the Persian period.[2]

Our conclusion must be that the language of Ecclesiastes does not at present provide an adequate resource for dating. It is possible that a particular style was adopted for pessimism literature. The possibility that a northern dialect of Hebrew was used must be left open. Equally it is possible that its dialect is Phoenicianizing. Certainly no other document possesses precisely the same characteristics, and no reliable date can be given this way. The language of Ecclesiastes is probably of interest more in dialectology than chronology.

[1] There is evidence that ancient documents could be lightly updated with old-fashioned words replaced. *Cf.* K. A. Kitchen, *Ancient Orient and Old Testament* (1966), pp. 141–143.

[2] *Cf.* M. H. Pope's similar remark concerning *pardes* in the Song of Songs. Although he does not regard that book as entirely early, yet he does not feel any weight can be given to its inclusion of *pardes* (*cf. Song of Songs* (1977), p. 31). G. Archer believes the words derive from Sanskrit (*A Survey of Old Testament Introduction* (1964), p. 470).

ECCLESIASTES

Greek influence

A second factor is the question of the book's dependence on early Greek writings. It is virtually certain that the Preacher had some knowledge of and interacted with ancient Near Eastern pessimism,[1] but what of similar Greek writings? The theory put forward by Zirkel in 1792, that Greek influence could be detected in the *language* of Ecclesiastes, is now almost universally abandoned.[2] Reviewing the question in 1925 H. Ranston[3] concluded that there was evidence of dependence on Theognis and Hesiod. In that case Ecclesiastes should probably be dated after the death of Alexander (323 BC), when Hellenistic culture increasingly spread throughout the ancient world.

More recently scholars have been less inclined to trace Greek influence. O. Loretz finds none at all.[4] Others (*e.g.* J. Bright[5]) see only a general and indirect influence. M. Hengel[6] concedes that all attempts to prove dependence on particular Greek writers (*e.g.* Epicurus, Heraclitus, Hesiod, Theognis) have failed. Yet, dating Ecclesiastes between 270 and 220 BC, he agrees with R. Kroeber that 'in ideas and mood the work has contacts with the spirit of Hellenism'.[7] Hengel admits that the Greek parallels adduced for the book are unsatisfactory and that 'because of the "international" spread of wisdom and its universal themes the indication of parallels says nothing about their origin'. He also dismisses attempts to find Graecisms in particular words. However, he feels that the Preacher's spirit is Greek: his individualistic critical analysis of experience, his cool detachment towards the correction of injustice, his universal rather than distinctively Israelite conception of God, his willingness to criticize orthodox Judaism, are all thought to reflect a Hellenistic outlook.

Hengel's argument, however, presumes that Ecclesiastes is definitely a third-century work. If that assumption is correct, to

[1] *Cf.* O. Loretz, *Qohelet und der Alte Orient* (1964) for Mesopotamian contacts; and P. Humbert, *Recherches sur les sources Égyptiennes de la Littérature Sapientale d'Israël* (1929), for Egyptian contacts. Humbert perhaps overstates his case.

[2] It was upheld by various scholars in the late nineteenth century; see C. C. Forman, *JSS*, 3, 1958, pp. 336f.

[3] H. Ranston, *Ecclesiastes and the Early Greek Wisdom Literature* (1925).

[4] O. Loretz, *Qohelet und der Alte Orient*, pp. 45–57. Cyrus Gordon also speaks of 'the complete absence of Greek influence', *IEJ*, 5, 1955, p. 87.

[5] J. Bright, *A History of Israel* (²1972), p. 452.

[6] M. Hengel, *Judaism and Hellenism* (1974), vol. 1, pp. 115–128; vol. 2, pp. 77–87.

[7] *Ibid.*, vol. 1, p. 116; *cf.* R. Kroeber, *Der Prediger* (1963), p. 47.

see Hellenistic atmosphere in the book may well be right. But the argument is circular. No convincing evidence for influence by Greek authors has been produced, other than the assumption that Ecclesiastes is to be dated in the third century.

There are reasons, however, for caution in seeing Greek influence in the Preacher's work. Many of the parallels cited are trivial and could be found anywhere in the ancient Near East. Our ignorance of the future, the claim to more than ordinary wisdom, the dependence of mankind upon God or the gods, the apparent inconsistency of earthly retribution – these themes, common to Ecclesiastes, Theognis and Hesiod, are found throughout the ancient Near East. The parallels are more likely part of a common stock of wisdom subject-matter than specific borrowings. By contrast, the God-centred, judgment-orientated, contented life held forth in Ecclesiastes is very different from the bleak sensualism of Theognis. Pessimism concerning human life and destiny appears from the third millennium onwards. It is likely that both the Greeks and Ecclesiastes knew of it; there is no need to postulate that the Preacher drew upon Greek literature. Certainly Ecclesiastes cannot be reliably dated on these grounds.[1]

Internal claims

Ecclesiastes is not only a collection of wisdom material; it is also a narrative.[2] Within its pages there is a person who unobtrusively appears in the words 'says the Preacher'. At the very beginning (Ec. 1:2) we are gently informed that one man is reporting the wisdom material of another man. Roughly in the middle (7:27), the words appear again as a delicate reminder. At the end (12:8), lest we have forgotten, they appear again. Around this narrative is added a title (1:1) and an epilogue (12:9–14).

Who are the two personages within the book? Is one man presenting the work of another? Or is a man presenting himself and adopting the dual role of wise man and editor of his own material? There are slight pointers in both directions. On the

[1] F. Dornseiff also argued for ancient Near Eastern influences upon Hesiod (cf. *Kleine Schriften*, I. *Antike und Alter Orient* (1956), pp. 72–95). P. Walcot compares themes which Hesiod's *Works and Days* has in common with the Egyptian *Instructions of 'Onchsheshonqy* ('Hesiod and the Instructions of 'Onchsheshonqy', *JNES*, 21, 1962, pp. 215–219).
[2] For this point, cf. the stimulating article by Michael V. Fox, 'Frame-Narrative and Composition in the Book of Qoheleth', *HUCA*, 48, 1977, pp. 83–106.

one hand the voice that says 'says the Preacher' would most naturally be taken as distinct from the author of the material; he would be an editor presenting the material of a revered wise man. Leaving aside 1:2; 7:27; 12:8, the Preacher speaks of himself not in the third person but in the first. Although 1:2 and 12:8 could be self-introduction and self-commendation, the intrusive 'says the Preacher' would be pointless in 7:27 unless the speaker at that instant is a second person peeping through the curtain. As Fox says: 'While one can speak of himself in the third person, it is unlikely he would do so in the middle of a first-person sentence.'

On the other hand, even within so small a compass as 12:9–14 there are phrases which exactly echo the style and phraseology of the bulk of the book. The use of *uťyōṭēr* (12:9, 11; *cf.* 7:11, *etc.*), his way of speaking of 'the people' (12:9; *cf.* 4:16), the 'master of…' idiom (in the Heb. of 12:11; *cf.* 10:11, 20 and slightly differently in 5:10, 12; 8:18), each echoes the style of the bulk of the material. Delitzsch points to the similarity of the structure in 12:9–11; 1:7 and 6:5.

The hypothesis (and it can be no more than that), which accounts for these phenomena, is that an editor is presenting *in his own words and style* the teaching of a revered wise man. The revered teacher is 'the Preacher' (Heb. *Qōhelet*); the editor-author presenting Qoheleth's wisdom is an unnamed and unknown admirer or disciple working at a date and location that cannot be precisely determined. Thus one style pervades the book; but two people, Qoheleth the originator of the material and an unnamed author-editor, lay behind it.

Who then is Qoheleth and why is this enigmatic name used? The phrases 'son of David, king[1] in Jerusalem' (1:1) and 'king over Israel' (1:12) point clearly to Solomon. Admittedly 'son of David' could describe any descendant of David. Many generations after the king a certain Hattush is described as 'of the sons of David' (Ezr. 8:2). It is also true that after the fall of Samaria (722 BC), and even sporadically before, 'Israel' might be applied to the southern kingdom Judah. In theory, therefore, any later

[1] H. L. Ginsberg (*Studies in Koheleth*, 1950, pp. 12ff.; *WIANE*, p. 149) takes *mlk* to be not *melek* (king) but *mōlek*, which he renders 'a property-owner', citing an Arabic verb meaning 'to own'. W. F. Albright takes it as *mōlēk* or *mallāk*, which is translated 'counsellor' on the basis of the Aramaic verb *mlk* 'to counsel' (*WIANE*, p. 15). Although these hypotheses are attractive, they remain but conjectures. There is no evidence for deleting 'over Israel' for 1:12, over which both theories stumble.

Davidic king could have been the author. Nevertheless, in view of the traditions concerning Solomon (1 Ki. 2–12; 2 Ch. 1–9), without further definition the title would certainly lead any reader to suppose that the allusion is to him. Also the account in 2:1–11 is strongly reminiscent of Solomon; almost every phrase has its parallel in the narratives concerning Solomon. B. Porten points out the the root *qhl* serves to mark the beginning and end of several of the units of narrative in 1 Kings 8.[1]

However, there are indications that Solomon himself was not the author. Not only is the presenter of the material apparently distinct from Qoheleth: the name Solomon is avoided. *Qōheleṯ* (1:1f., 12; 7:27; 12:8–10, normally translated 'Preacher') is probably an entirely artificial name. The root *qhl* is used of 'gathering' or 'assembling' people but not of collecting things. Names with similar structure (*sōp̄ereṯ*, 'scribe', Ezr. 2:55; *pōḵereṯ*, 'binder', Ne. 7:59) are personal, yet appear to have derived from titles. One might compare in English Baker or Smith, both names and occupations. There are verbal forms *niqhal* ('to assemble, be gathered') and *hiqhîl* ('to gather an assembly'). Thus it is likely that *Qōheleṯ* is a name meaning 'one who gathers an assembly to address it', yet retaining an official force so that it can be used with the article: 'the *Qōheleṯ*' (7:27). The meaning is easily seen in 1 Kings 8:1, where Solomon gathers (*qhl*) the people of Israel for worship, prayer and instruction.[2] 'Preacher' is as good a translation as any.

We may conclude that the author is a pseudo-editor, an editor-author, writing in defence of faith in the God of Israel. He is an admirer of Solomon, writing up the lessons of Solomon's life in the tradition of the wisdom for which Solomon was famous. Yet Ecclesiastes is not pseudonymous, and the writer avoids using Solomon's name. Instead he portrays his material as coming from 'Mr Preacher', who has all the characteristics of Solomon except his name. The epilogue portraying Qoheleth has all the appearances of referring to an actual historical character: a wise man, a collector of proverbs, a teacher and writer. Who else but Solomon? Avoidance of the name must

---

[1] B. Porten, 'The Structure and Theme of the Solomon Narrative (1 Kings 3–11)', *HUCA*, 38, 1967, pp. 93–128.

[2] On this view the qal form of *Qōheleṯ* is the equivalent to the hiphil. The tendency of the qal to take over the functions of derived conjugations is especially noticeable in later Mishnaic Hebrew (*cf.* M. H. Segal, *A Grammar of Mishnaic Hebrew* (1927), p. 56).

stem from the fact that the editor-author puts things in his own way and declines to foist a work directly on Solomon. Yet he thinks of the material as Solomon's; it is what Solomon would have said had he addressed himself to the subject of pessimism. The artificiality of the name Qoheleth was probably conspicuous. It is as though there were a book under the pen-name of 'John Smith, King of England' which proceeded to press home some lessons from the viewpoint of an English monarch. The story is real enough; it is Solomon's with its major lessons highlighted. But Qoheleth was honest enough to sign himself (for so we might paraphrase): 'Mr Preacher, King of Israel.'

The date of the book must be left undecided. If it contains significant Persian words, then it must be dated after the fifth century. If, however, as is likely, the Iranian words are not determinative of date, the matter must be left open until more is known of the unique dialect in which the book is written.[1]

III. THE CANONICITY OF ECCLESIASTES

We may distinguish between inherent canonicity and recognition of canonicity. If any part of Scripture is authoritative as coming from God, it was so from the moment of its being written or of its coming to its final literary form. Recognition of that authority is a distinct issue.[2]

Canonicity in early times
Comparatively little is known of the stages by which the Old

---

[1] In arguing for a late date other points that are often mentioned are: *i.* the identification of historical incidents within the book (*cf.* 4:13–16; 9:14–15); *ii.* the reflection of post-exilic decadent society in the Preacher's arguments; *iii.* the occasions when the Preacher refers critically to kingship, and the mention of kings 'before me in Jerusalem' (1:16; 2:9). None of these arguments is very weighty and they are best left aside. No agreement has been reached concerning any historical event behind 4:13–16; 9:14–15. To date the kind of society the Preacher was addressing is a very subjective matter; the argument addresses itself to mankind's plight at any time. There were kings in Jerusalem before Solomon, and in any case it is wisdom not kingship that is mentioned in 1:16; 2:9. For these arguments, *cf.* E. J. Young, *Introduction to the Old Testament* (1960), pp. 367–369; H. H. Rowley, *The Growth of the Old Testament* (1950), pp. 152–154.

[2] *Cf.* E. J. Young, 'The canon of the Old Testament' in C. F. H. Henry (ed.), *Revelation and the Bible* (1959), pp. 153–168. For a consideration of the significance of canon emphasizing 'the peculiar relationship between text and people of God which is constitutive of the canon', *cf.* B. S. Childs, *Introduction to the Old Testament as Scripture* (1979), pp. 46–103.

Testament books were publicly recognized as canonical. S. Z. Leiman defines as canonical 'a book accepted by Jews as authoritative for religious practice and/or doctrine, and whose authority is binding upon the Jewish people for all generations [and which is] to be studied and expounded in private and in public'.[1] Defined thus, indications of the canonicity of Ecclesiastes begin in the early second century BC. Ben Sira is the earliest writer to use it, although not indicating how he viewed its status.[2] The preface to the Greek translation refers to 'the law, the prophets and the other books of our fathers', which may well include Ecclesiastes in the last part of this triad. Leiman thinks that 2 Maccabees 2:14f. may describe the closing of the canon of the hagiographa: 'Judah collected all the books that had been lost on account of the war.'[3] But it would be wise not to read too much into this.

The pseudepigraphical IV Ezra (final redaction AD 100) contains the first explicit reference to the twenty-four books of the Old Testament, Samuel, Kings, Twelve Prophets, Chronicles, Ezra-Nehemiah constituting one each. In the first century AD Josephus refers to a tri-partite canon of twenty-two books, apparently counting Jeremiah-Lamentations and Judges-Ruth as also one book each. He explicitly mentions 'four books' which 'contain hymns to God': Psalms, Proverbs, Ecclesiastes and Song of Songs.[4]

The canon of the Qumran community cannot perhaps be adequately assessed, but it is noteworthy that the sectaries possessed and used Ecclesiastes.[5]

The New Testament also provides evidence of the existence in the first century AD of a tri-partite canon. The word 'psalms' in Luke 24:44 probably refers to the entire hagiographa, although Ecclesiastes is nowhere explicitly mentioned in the New Testament. Early Christian writers who explicitly mention Ecclesiastes in lists of canonical books of Scripture include Melito, bishop of Sardis (*c.* AD 170), Origen (*c.* AD 185–225), Epiphanius,

[1] S. Z. Leiman, *The Canonization of the Hebrew Scriptures: The Talmudic and Midrashic Evidence* (1976), p. 14.

[2] For links between Ben Sira and Ecclesiastes, *cf.* T. Middendorp, *Die Stellung Jesu Ben Siras zwischen Judentum und Hellenismus* (1973), pp. 35–90.

[3] S. Z. Leiman, *op. cit.*, p. 29.

[4] *Against Apion* 1.37–43.

[5] For possible evidence of use of Ecclesiastes in the Thanksgiving Hymns, *cf.* I. H. Eybers' comments in S. Z. Leiman (ed.), *The Canon and Masorah of the Hebrew Bible* (1974), p.23..

ECCLESIASTES

bishop of Sardis (*c.* AD 315 – 403), Jerome (*c.* AD 347 – 419).[1]

Among early Jewish writers an anonymous, undated Talmudic text, Baba Bathra 14b–15a, assumes a threefold division of canonical Scripture and includes Ecclesiastes explicitly. Several rabbinic texts (*e.g.* Bemidhbar Rabbah 14:4; Koheleth Rabbah 12:12) take Ecclesiastes 12:12 ('Beyond these...be careful') as a caution against reading books outside the inspired twenty-four.

Leiman cites evidence that second-century rabbis disputed whether the prophets and the writings were equal in status; the majority argued that they were.[2] Sifre on Deuteronomy considers Ecclesiastes as authoritative as Amos or Jeremiah on the grounds of its Solomonic authorship. 'It is written: *The words of Amos*...Similarly it is written: *The words of Qoheleth*...Is this all that Solomon prophesied? Did he not compose three books, half his wisdom in parables?'

In the third century AD Rabbi Joshua ben Levi is said to have urged the same viewpoint: 'The holy spirit rested on him, and he composed three books: Proverbs, Ecclesiastes and the Song of Songs.' Leiman argues from the early rabbinic evidence that, in contrast to medieval Jewish ideas, 'neither degree of sanctity nor mode of inspiration separate "Writings" from "Prophets", for the terms "prophecy" and "holy spirit" are used interchangeably when describing books from either the Prophets or the Hagiographa'.[3]

The conflicting statements within Ecclesiastes evidently made some query its canonical status. In Shabbath 30b we are told that a third-century rabbi had said: 'The sages wished to withdraw the book of Ecclesiastes because its words are self-contradictory... The book of Proverbs they wished to withdraw because its statements are self-contradictory. Yet why did they not withdraw it? They said: Did we not examine the book of Ecclesiastes and find a reconciliation?' Similarly the Aboth of Rabbi Nathan 1:4 tells us that a second-century rabbi had said that Ecclesiastes was at one time temporarily withdrawn until its statement had been interpreted. In the second century AD Rabbi Simeon and Rabbi Jose reported disputes over the canonicity of Ecclesiastes, denied by the school of Hillel and affirmed by the school of

---

[1] *Cf.* S. Z. Leiman, *The Canonization of the Hebrew Scriptures*, pp. 41–50 for details.

[2] *Ibid.*, pp. 60–64.

[3] *Ibid.*, p. 66. I translate the Hebrew words in this quotation.

Shammai.[1] Nevertheless, Baba ben Buta, a distinguished Shammaite, expounded Ecclesiastes publicly.[2]

It has often been maintained that Ecclesiastes, along with other books of the Hagiographa, was adopted into the canon at the Synod of Jamnia in AD 100.[3] The evidence, however, does not seem to warrant precisely this construction. Rabbinical discussions revolve not around *whether* Ecclesiastes was canonical, but *why* it was. Jamnia discussed only books already considered canonical; none was treated as a candidate for admission.[4]

Canonicity today

Within its pages Ecclesiastes claims that its wisdom comes from 'one Shepherd', and that beyond its wisdom the would-be wise man must exercise care (12:11f.). It is doubtful that the 'one Shepherd' is Solomon or the author. This would imply a scepticism of all wisdom except the Preacher's, which is unlikely to be the author's view. The 'one Shepherd' is surely God. Here we have an unobtrusive claim to inspiration, a first step towards the New Testament claim that all Scripture, including Ecclesiastes, is 'God-breathed' (2 Tim. 3:16).

The question of the canonicity of Ecclesiastes involves the validity of this claim, and is theological and personal as well as historical. What elicits recognition of any part of Scripture as inherently authoritative? A certain circularity is inevitable, whatever one's position. The person who is hostile to claims for authority in any religious document will bring his presuppositions to Ecclesiastes and find his doubts confirmed. Another person who comes to the Bible, perhaps to Ecclesiastes, with openness is ready to hear and find that the Preacher speaks to him as never before. Both have travelled in a circle — the latter perhaps in a spiral, for his position is higher than before.

Six factors may contribute to the recognition of inspiration in any document of Scripture: (i) its place in the history of redemption; (ii) its authorship or authorship associations; (iii) its content; (iv) its preservation; (v) the testimony of the church; (vi) the witness of the Spirit. There can be little doubt that

---

[1] *Cf.* the rabbinic texts M. Eduyoth 5:3 and M. Yadayim 3:5.
[2] S. Z. Leiman, *op. cit.*, p. 112.
[3] *E.g.* H. E. Ryle, *The Canon of the Old Testament* (1892), p. 173.
[4] *Cf.* R. C. Newman, 'The Council of Jamnia and the Old Testament Canon', *WTJ*, 38, 1975–6, pp. 319–349; J. E. Goldingay, *Approaches to Old Testament Interpretation* (1981), pp. 139–145.

ECCLESIASTES

Ecclesiastes' association with Solomon contributed to its recognition. The realization that Solomon may not be its final author need detract less from this than might be thought; just as some New Testament books were 'apostolic' without apostles for authors, so Ecclesiastes is clearly in some sense 'Solomonic' without being directly produced by him. Ecclesiastes emerges within a history of redemption in association with a wisdom-tradition beginning with Solomon. Its providential emergence in such circumstances demands our consideration.

In the final analysis, however, it will be the message that grips us. Some will have ears, but will not hear. Others will say, 'We will hear you again about this' (Acts 17:32). Yet others will say, 'No man ever spoke like this man!' (Jn. 7:46).

IV. ECCLESIASTES IN ITS ANCIENT NEAR EASTERN SETTING

Ecclesiastes is an Israelite sample of a literary tradition, widely attested in the ancient Near East, known as 'wisdom literature'. In the late third and early second millennium BC, the Sumerians committed to writing a rich body of literature, among which we find riddles, collections of proverbs, and reflective essays large and small.

Short proverbs include sayings that pre-echo our own 'Blood is thicker than water' and 'Out of the frying pan into the fire'. The Sumerian equivalents are: 'Friendship lasts a day, kinship lasts for ever' and 'Upon my escaping from the wild-ox, the wild cow confronted me'.[1]

Larger works include a poetic essay reconstructed from five tablets and fragments, which deals with the problem of suffering in a way reminiscent of the book of Job:

> You have doled out to me suffering ever new,
> I entered the house, heavy is the spirit,
> I, the same man, went out to the street, oppressed is
>   the heart,
> With me, the valiant, my righteous shepherd has become
>   angry, has looked upon me inimically,
> My herdsman has sought out evil forces against me who
>   am not (his enemy),
> My companion says not a true word to me,
> My friend gives the lie to my righteous word.[2]

[1] S. N. Kramer, *History Begins at Sumer* (1961), pp. 181–182.
[2] *Cf. ANET*, p. 590; S. N. Kramer, '"Man and his God". A Sumerian

Another Sumerian work, the *Instructions of Suruppak*, dates from 2200 BC or earlier and is known also in Old Babylonian (1800 BC?) and later Babylonian (1100 BC?) versions.[1]

Babylon perpetuated the tradition with its series of fables,[2] and its 'Babylonian Job', *Ludlul Bel Nemeqi*, which was a variation of a tale going back to the second millennium at least,[3] as well as its less argumentative *Counsels of Wisdom*[4] and the Babylonian version of the *Instructions of Suruppak*.[5] At a still later date we have the *Words of Ahikar*, known primarily in a fifth-century Aramaic version but with an Assyrian setting dating from the days of Sennacherib and Esarhaddon (7th century BC),[6] and the *Advice to a Prince* dated between 1000 and 700 BC.[7] D. J. Wiseman mentions also quotations from fables and parables in letters from Old Babylonian times (*c.* 1700 BC) to the seventh century BC.[8]

Studies of Eblaite wisdom have yet to be made available; but it is clear that Ebla too in the late third millennium BC already had its share of parables, riddles and fables associated with wisdom writings.[9] Evidence of early written wisdom is also found in the El Amarna letters of the fourteenth century BC, where Canaanite overlords quote proverbial sayings in letters to Pharaohs. From the thirteenth-century Ugarit comes the *Instructions of Sube-Awelim* in Akkadian and Hittite.[10]

A similar stream of wisdom writings is found in Egypt. In the

---

variation on the "Job" motif', *WIANE*, pp. 170–182. See further 'The First Proverbs and Sayings', ch. 16 in S. N. Kramer, *History Begins at Sumer* (1961); E. I. Gordon, *Sumerian Proverbs* (1959), pp. 1–21; J. J. A. van Dijk, *La sagesse sumero-accadienne* (1953). For a recent guide to available texts of 'Instructional' wisdom books, *cf.* K. A. Kitchen, 'Proverbs and Wisdom Books of the Ancient Near East', *TB*, 28, 1977, esp. pp. 111–114.

[1] *Cf.* D. J. Wiseman, 'Israel's Literary Neighbours in the 13th Century B.C.', *JNSL*, 5, 1977, esp. p. 85; B. Alster, *The Instructions of Suruppak* (1974). Alster dates the earliest Sumerian version from Abu Salabikh even earlier, at 2500 BC.

[2] *Cf.* Lambert, pp. 21–62.

[3] D. J. Wiseman (*art. cit.*, p. 83) refers to an unpublished text to be dated before 1100 BC , which has often been the date given to this text.

[4] *Cf.* Lambert, pp. 96-107.

[5] *Cf.* Lambert, pp. 92–95; B. Alster, *op. cit.*

[6] *Cf. ANET*, pp. 427–430; A. E. Cowley, *Aramaic Papyri of the Fifth Century B.C.* (1923), pp. 204–228.

[7] *Cf.* Lambert, pp. 110–115.

[8] D. J. Wiseman, *art. cit.*, p. 89.

[9] *Cf.* G. Pettinato, *Orientalia*, 44, 1975, pp. 361–374.

[10] *Cf.* D. J. Wiseman, *art. cit.*, p. 85; C. F. A. Schaeffer (ed.), *Ugaritica V* (1963), pp. 273–290, 779–784.

middle of the third millennium BC a change from oral to literary wisdom led to a succession of wisdom writings. Written between 2700 and 2400 BC, the *Instruction of Imhotep*,[1] the *Instruction of Ptah-hotep*,[2] the *Instruction of Kegemni*,[3] and the *Instruction of Hardidief*[4] consist of compilations of wise sayings. The tradition continues in the *Instruction of Ani*[5] and the *Instruction of Amenemopet*,[6] probably written between the eleventh and tenth centuries BC. More sustained and argumentative are the social protest of *The Eloquent Peasant*,[7] the theology of the *Divine Attributes of Pharaoh*,[8] and the meditation *In Praise of Learned Scribes*.[9]

These works and others constitute the 'wisdom writings' of the ancient Near East. The Old Testament itself testifies to the international character of wisdom in its references to the wisdom of Egypt (Gn. 41:8; Ex. 7:11–12; 1 Ki. 4:30; Is. 19:11–12), Edom (Je. 49:7; Ob. 8), Arabia (Pr. 30:1; 31:1; and the story of the Queen of Sheba), Phoenicia (Ezk. 27:8–9; 28:4–7, 12, 17; Zc. 9:2), 'the East' (1 Ki. 4:30), Babel (Is. 47:10; Je. 50:35; 51:57; Dn. 1:20; 2:2, 10, 12–14, 18, 24, 27, 48; 5:7–8, 11, 15) and Persia (Est. 1:13; 6:13).

In Israel the techniques of the wisdom writers were known and used from earliest days. The fables of Jotham (Jdg. 9:7–15), the riddle of Samson (Jdg. 14:12ff.), the epigrams concerning Saul (1 Sa. 10:12) and David (1 Sa. 18:7), the 'proverb of the ancients' (1 Sa. 24:13), the parable of Nathan (2 Sa. 12:1–4) and of the woman of Tekoa (2 Sa. 14:5ff.) all reflect the wise man's art. Solomon, however, gave Israel's wisdom its greatest impetus (1 Ki. 2:6; 3:28; 4:29–34; 5:7, 12; 10:1–13; 11:41; 2 Ch. 1:7–12; 9:1–12). Of his literary output there remain only Proverbs (in part), possibly the Song of Songs and probably Psalms 72 and 127.[10]

We may itemize at least seven possible sources of the wisdom

[1] *Cf.* G. Posener, *Revue d'Egyptologie*, 6, 1949, p. 31.
[2] *Cf. ANET*, pp. 412–414.
[3] *Cf.* M. Lichtheim, *Ancient Egyptian Literature*, vol. 1 (1973), pp. 59–61.
[4] *Cf. ANET*, pp. 419–420.   [5] *Cf. ANET*, pp. 420–421.
[6] *Cf. ANET*, pp. 421–425.   [7] *Cf. ANET*, pp. 407–410.
[8] *Cf. ANET*, p. 431.   [9] *Cf. ANET*, pp. 431–432.
[10] The Solomonic origin of these works and of the wisdom tradition as a whole is a matter of dispute. R. B. Y. Scott argues ('Solomon and the Beginnings of Wisdom in Israel', *WIANE*, pp. 262–279) that the traditions concerning Solomon are unreliable. But royal patronage of wisdom was well known centuries before Solomon, and it is needlessly sceptical to query the reliability of the 1 Kings

INTRODUCTION

of Israel, following some suggestions of R. B. Y. Scott.[1] These
are: (i) the accumulated folk-wisdom of Israel's culture; (ii) the
educational processes in home and later in schools; (iii) the
emergence of gifted counsellors whose advice was sought by
both common people and kings; (iv) the intellectual curiosity
and moral concern of individuals; (v) the institutionalization of
wisdom through a scribal profession associated with the temple
and the court; (vi) a growing body of Israelite wisdom writings
and collected proverbs which would be the object of further
meditation and accumulation of further wisdom; (vii) contact
with the wisdom of surrounding cultures, some of whose wisdom
might be welcomed into the body of Israel's tradition, at the
same time receiving to a lesser or greater degree the stamp of
Israel's own covenant faith.

It is difficult to assess the precise extent of Israel's debt to the
wisdom of surrounding nations. For example, the alleged and
much-cited dependence of Proverbs on the *Instruction of Amenemope*
is not securely based.[2] There are certainly parallels between
Mesopotamian, Egyptian and Canaanite wisdom; but Israel
had traditions of her own which parted company with the
thought of surrounding nations. The Solomon narrative (*cf.*
1 Ki. 4:30) refers to such non-Israelite wisdom but claims that
Israel's wisdom outstripped that of surrounding nations. We
must be ready, therefore, to find both parallels and major
differences. Solomon was prepared to use the skills of surrounding peoples to build a temple for the Lord (1 Ki. 5:6–12, 18;
7:14; 2 Ch. 2:17), but he imposed on it a distinctive structure
(1 Ki. 6:14–38). We must be ready to see something similar in
wisdom literature. The materials and the workmen may come
from anywhere, but the over-all content will be in honour of the

narrative. For a more positive approach urging that 1 Ki. 3–11 faithfully reflects
the age of Solomon, *cf.* B. Porten, 'The Structure and Theme of the Solomon
Narrative (1 Kings 3–11)', *HUCA*, 38, 1967, pp. 93–128. For the authorship of
Song of Songs, *cf.* the brief survey of opinions in M. H. Pope, *Song of Songs* (1977),
pp. 22–33. Among those who have argued for a Solomonic or near-Solomonic
date are M. H. Segal, C. Rabin, G. Gerleman. Others feel that the Song contains
Solomonic material although its final redaction is later (R. Gordis, W. F.
Albright). *Cf.* M. H. Pope, *loc. cit.*, for details and references.
[1] *Cf.* R. B. Y. Scott, 'The Study of the Wisdom Literature', *Interpretation*, 24,
1970, pp. 20–45, esp. p. 29.
[2] The recent study by J. Ruffle argues persuasively that the connections are
not as significant as has often been thought. *Cf.* 'The Teaching of Amenemope
and its Connection with the Book of Proverbs', *TB*, 28, 1977, pp. 29–68.

God of Israel. Israelite writers were not above using contemporary literary forms to express their own God-given message.

Among the links between wisdom and Israel's faith, D. A. Hubbard mentions: (i) the relationship between the establishing of the monarchy and the rise of a wisdom literary tradition; (ii) the wisdom techniques used by prophets in the propagation of their distinctive faith; (iii) the links between wisdom and law seen in connections between Proverbs and Deuteronomy; (iv) the occurrence of wisdom motifs in the Psalter; and (v) the attributes of wisdom in the stories of Joseph.[1] To these we may add the Israelite viewpoint in much of the content and setting of the wisdom writings. Although Proverbs, for example, is not above using purely mundane arguments (*e.g.* Pr. 6:6–11), yet there are editorial references to Solomon, David, and Israel (1:1), to Hezekiah and Judah (25:1). Within the body of the book there are allusions to the fear of Yahweh (1:7, 29, *etc.*), to Yahweh's giving wisdom (2:6, *etc.*), to 'the covenant of her God' (2:17), to God's commandments (3:1) and the 'assembled congregation' (5:14). In Ecclesiastes, although specially Israelite themes are not prominent, for the writer's argument is designed to have universal appeal, yet we have passing references to David, Jerusalem and Israel (1:1, 12, 16; 2:7, 9), thirty-two references to '*the* God', allusions to the temple and the fulfilment of a vow there, and to the peace-offering (5:1–7), all of which are Israelite overtones.

'Wisdom' has many facets. Scholars have often attempted to distinguish between different types of wisdom, different stages in its development, and different contexts in which it occurs. Von Rad[2] and McKane[3] identify an 'old wisdom' which von Rad regards as a blend of anthropocentricity and piety, but which McKane regards as the sagacity and 'disciplined empiricism' of royal counsellors arising in the days of David and Solomon. Crenshaw distinguishes between family/clan wisdom, court wisdom and scribal wisdom.[4] It was also once the fashion to distinguish between 'simple' early wisdom and developed or complex 'late' wisdom, including personification of wisdom

---

[1] *Cf.* 'The Wisdom Movement and Israel's Covenant Faith', *TB*, 17, 1966, pp. 3–33.
[2] *Cf.* G. von Rad, *Wisdom in Israel* (1972); *Old Testament Theology*, vol. 1 (1962), pp. 418–459.
[3] *Cf.* W. McKane, *Prophets and Wise Men* (1965); *Proverbs* (1970), pp. 10–22.
[4] *Cf. SIAIW*, p. 3.

itself.[1] However, personification of wisdom antedates Solomon.[2] The idea of a linear evolvement of wisdom must be, and very largely has been, abandoned.[3]

A full and satisfying survey of the various aspects of wisdom in the Old Testament has yet to be produced.[4] Suffice it to say that the wisdom of the Old Testament can be considered from the viewpoints of (i) its level of prestige (ranging from folk-wisdom to courtly wisdom); (ii) its content (ranging from practical maxims to theological epics such as Job); (iii) its practitioners (ranging from the common man, through recognized 'wise men', to royal patrons); (iv) its validity (for there are warnings about false wisdom within the pages of the Old Testament); (v) its stages of development; and (vi) its particular literary techniques.

But such distinctions must not be pressed too far. Old Testament wisdom writings claim royal patronage, while showing great concern for and relevance to the common people of Israel. There is no reason to suspect the accuracy of this presentation. Royal patronage of wisdom was centuries old in the ancient Near East by the time of Solomon. The responsibility of king and courtiers towards the common people is part of Israel's heritage. To drive a wedge between courtly and humble wisdom contradicts the claims of the material we are handling. Such distinctions are in emphasis only, nuanced and not rigid.

The royal wisdom of the reign of Solomon was also a nature wisdom according to the picture we have in the Solomon narrative. 'Wisdom' in the Old Testament is so diversified and all-embracing that it almost ceases to be a useful term; more than one scholar prefers to avoid it altogether.[5] It encompasses technical and artistic ability, native cunning, devout piety, magical craft, experienced statesmanship. In one setting it will be highly praised; in another severely denounced.

The particular brand of wisdom that characterizes Eccle-

---

[1] *Cf.* S. R. Driver, *An Introduction to the Literature of the Old Testament* (1913), p. 406; W. O. E. Oesterley and T. H. Robinson, *An Introduction to the Books of the Old Testament* (1934), pp. 205–207.

[2] *Cf.* K. A. Kitchen, *Ancient Orient and Old Testament* (1966), p. 127, esp. n. 57.

[3] *Cf.* K. A. Kitchen, 'Proverbs and Wisdom Books of the Ancient Near East: The Factual History of a Literary Form', *TB*, 28, 1977, pp. 69–114.

[4] J. L. Crenshaw surveys briefly the main studies of wisdom in English (*Old Testament Wisdom* (1982), pp. 11f.).

[5] *Cf.* R. N. Whybray, *The Intellectual Tradition in the Old Testament* (1974); J. L. Crenshaw, *SIAIW*, pp. 4, 37.

siastes is well attested in the ancient world. We may call it 'pessimism literature'. Ecclesiastes is the only biblical example of this old literary tradition. In an Egyptian work, *The Man Who Was Tired of Life*, written between 2300 and 2100 BC, a man disputed with his soul whether life was worth living or whether suicide was the only logical act. 'Life is a transitory state,' he complained to himself; 'you are alive but what profit do you get? Yet you yearn for life like a man of wealth.' Death is 'a bringer of weeping'; never again afterwards will a man 'see the sun'. Little can be done. 'Follow the happy day and forget care.'[1] Similar is the Egyptian *Song of the Harper* (*c.* 2100 BC) which contains striking parallels to Ecclesiastes. The transitoriness of man troubles the poet. 'Generations pass away and others remain...' (*cf.* Ec. 1:4). So he calls his hearers to surrender to pleasure while they can:

> Let thy desire flourish,
> In order to let thy heart forget the beautifications for
>   thee [*i.e.* funeral preparations]
> Follow thy desire, as long as thou shalt live.
> Put myrrh upon thy head and clothing of fine linen
>   upon thee,
> Being anointed with genuine marvels of the god's property.
> Set an increase to thy good things;
> Let not thy heart flag.
> Follow thy desire and thy good.
> Fulfil thy needs upon earth, after the command of thy heart,
> Until there come from thee, that day of mourning.

Death is irrevocable and throws a dark shadow over life.

> It is not given to man to take his property with him.
> Behold, there is not one who departs who comes back again![2]

The Babylonian *Counsels of a Pessimist* (of uncertain date,

---

[1] *Cf.* R. J. Williams, 'Reflections on the *Lebensmüde*', *JEA*, 48, 1962, pp. 49–56; R. O. Faulkner, 'The Man Who Tired Of Life', *JEA*, 42, 1956, pp. 21–40.

[2] *ANET*, p. 467. Other documents which give vent to depair or reflect on the purposelessness of life are *The Admonition of Ipuwer* (*ANET*, pp. 441–444), the *Discourse of Si-Sobek* of *c.* 2000 BC who complains 'This is the span of life; it is not known what may happen in it...' (J. W. B. Barns, *Five Ramesseum Papyri*, 1956, p. 4), *The Eloquent Peasant* (*ANET*, pp. 407–410), and *Instruction of Amen-Em-Opet*, ch. 18 (*ANET*, pp. 423–424).

anywhere between the 19th and 7th centuries BC) speaks in similar vein:

> (Whatever) men do does not last for ever
> Mankind and their achievements alike come to an end…
> Do (not) let evil sleep afflict your heart;
> Banish misery and suffering from your side;
> Misery and suffering produce a dream.

Its ending is fragmentary, but the gist is clear:

> Let (your) heart be quit of…remove…
> Your countenance…may (your face) smile…[1]

Likewise in the *Dialogue of Pessimism* (*c.* 1300 BC), a noble plans to do this or that but changes his mind. His servant gives reasons for or against. In the end the servant takes the initiative and declares that suicide is the only reasonable end. It is uncertain how seriously we should take the text, but eminent students of the ancient Near East (S. Langdon, R. J. Williams, W. G. Lambert, T. Jacobsen) have regarded it as an expression of the futility of all endeavour.[2]

'What then is good?' is the final question. Back comes the answer:

> To have my neck and your neck broken
> And to be thrown into the river is good.[3]

The Mesopotamian *Epic of Gilgamesh* contains similar sentiments, although its themes are wider than the pessimism literature generally. The *Epic* is known primarily in an Akkadian version of the seventh century BC; but Hurrian, Hittite and Sumerian fragments point to an earlier original, which may date from 2000 BC. The god Shamash states the problem:

> Gilgamesh, whither rovest thou?
> The life thou pursuest thou shalt not find.

Gilgamesh replies:

> After marching (and) roving over the steppe,
> Must I lay my head in the heart of the earth

[1] Lambert, p. 109. The brackets mark out uncertain text and translation.
[2] *Cf.* E. A. Speiser, 'The Case of the Obliging Servant', in *Oriental and Biblical Studies* (ed. J. J. Finkelstein and M. Greenberg, 1967), pp. 344–366. Speiser himself takes a different view.
[3] Lambert, p. 149.

That I may sleep through all the years?
Let mine eyes behold the sun
That I may have my fill of the light!
Darkness withdraws when there is enough light.
May one who indeed is dead behold yet the radiance
    of the sun![1]

Ecclesiastes stands in this tradition and concedes many of its contentions. Confine your viewpoint to this world and its resources, says the Preacher, and all the contentions of pessimism are true. The world is utterly pointless; good and bad die alike; the course of the world is inscrutable and futile; the wise man learns more from a funeral than a party.

Ecclesiastes, however, has another side, which we consider by looking briefly at ways commentators have tackled the enigmatic oscillations of his thought.

V. THE ENIGMA OF ECCLESIASTES

The major interpretative problem of Ecclesiastes is to understand its apparent internal contradictions and vicissitudes of thought. At times the Preacher seems to be gloomy, pessimistic, a skeleton at the feast; everything comes under his lashing scorn: laughter, drink, possessions, sex, work, wisdom, riches, honour, children, even righteousness. Yet, at other points he urges that we should enjoy life, that there is nothing better than to eat well, enjoy our labour, receive with gladness the riches God gives us but be content if he gives none. A man, he says, should seek wisdom and knowledge, drink his wine with a merry heart, and live joyfully with the wife whom he loves. The Preacher's argument and his relationship to Israelite orthodoxy seem ambiguous. At times he appears to overthrow everything Israel stood for; at other points we see the traditional views of God as sustainer and judge of all things, who gives life to men and who may be worshipped at Israel's focal point, the temple.

Thus one scholar describes the Preacher as 'a rationalist, an agnostic, a skeptic, a pessimist and a fatalist' (R. B. Y. Scott); others regard his work as orthodox (G. Ch. Aalders; H. C. Leupold) or as an indirect Messianic prophecy (H. W. Hertzberg).

Jewish commentators and early and medieval Christian

[1] *ANET*, p. 89.

36

writers often solved the problem by a spiritualizing exegesis. For example, Ecclesiastes 9:7 was interpreted by the Aramaic Targum as follows:

> 'The Lord of the world shall say to all the righteous one by one, Go taste with joy thy bread which has been given to thee on account of the bread which thou hast given to the poor and the unfortunate who were hungry, and drink with good heart thy wine, which is hidden for thee in the garden of Eden, for the wine which thou hast mingled for the poor and needy who were thirsty, for already thy good work has been pleasing before Jehovah.'[1]

Others viewed the oscillations of thought as a dialogue between two speakers. F. Yeard[2] maintained that the Preacher is interrupted by a sensual worldling or a refined sensualist, an approach adopted by J. Herder in 1778[3] and J. G. Eichhorn in 1779.[4]

Many have believed that the thought oscillates within the one writer's mind. Plumptre speaks of the 'oscillations and wanderings of thought by which the writer makes his way to his final conclusion'. C. H. Cornill felt that he was filled with doubts and perplexities, yet finally rose above them so that 'Old Testament piety nowhere enjoys a greater triumph than in the book of Koheleth…[He] falls back resignedly upon his childlike faith, in spite of the fact that it has proved itself inadequate to meet his perplexity'.[5]

Sometimes the Preacher is thought to present his pessimism for an evangelistic purpose. Since Nicolas de Lyra (c. 1270–1349) Christian orthodoxy has generally held that his purpose was to lift the heart to heavenly things by showing the futility of the world. This was the view of many Reformers and Puritans and their successors (Whitaker, Pemble, Cocceius, the 'Dutch Annotations', John Trapp, Matthew Poole, Matthew Henry).

---

[1] Cited by J. S. Wright, 'The Interpretation of Ecclesiastes', *EQ*, 18, 1946, p. 19. *Cf.* also S. Holm-Nielsen, 'On The Interpretation of Qoheleth in Early Christianity', *VT*, 24, 1974, pp. 168–177; *idem*, 'The Book of Ecclesiastes and the Interpretation of it in Jewish and Christian Theology', *ASTI*, 10, 1976, pp. 38–96.

[2] F. Yeard, *A Paraphrase Upon Ecclesiastes* (1701).

[3] Cited by Podechard, p. 143.

[4] *Cf.* a later statement in J. G. Eichhorn, *Einleitung in Das Alte Testament* (1803), vol. 3, pp. 650–655.

[5] C. H. Cornill, *Introduction to the Canonical Books of the Old Testament* (1907), pp. 451–452.

C. Bridges represents this tradition: 'We are permitted to taste the bitter wormwood of earthly streams, in order that, standing by the heavenly fountain, we may point our fellow sinners to the world of vanity we have left, and to the surpassing glory and delights of the world we have newly found'.[1] John Wesley[2] held a similar view; and this approach has retained its followers in more recent times, most notably E. W. Hengstenberg.

A modification of this view holds that 'This is the book of man "under the sun", reasoning about life; it is the best that man can do... Inspiration sets down accurately what passes, but the conclusions and reasonings are, after all, man's'.[3]

At the beginning of the twentieth century three scholars, A. H. McNeile in England, G. A. Barton in America and E. Podechard in France, took the view that Ecclesiastes was a sceptical work with considerable glossatorial additions. The additions, they believed, could be divided into two groups: one reflecting Israelite orthodoxy, the other adopting the viewpoint of a late wisdom writer. The approach was not entirely new. G. Bickell had maintained in 1884 that a book-form of Ecclesiastes had become confused and as a result extensive glosses were added.[4] P. Haupt considered only 124 of its 222 verses genuine.[5] D. C. Siegfried saw nine hands at work: five original authors, two epilogists and two editors.[6] These views, however, were regarded as extreme and not until McNeile, Barton and Podechard produced more restrained versions was the glossatorial approach taken seriously.

McNeile thought 1:1–2 and 12:8–10 to be editorial additions to an originally sceptical work, since (he argued) the work cannot be by Solomon and the original writer would not speak of himself in the third person. Eighteen passages, he felt, were added by a 'wise man', which he said were irrelevant to their context, or corrective of other parts of the book, or contrary in their 'frigid didactic style' to the heat and sting of the Preacher's complaints. Then he maintained that eleven passages were added by a pious Jew to bring the book into line with current orthodoxy.

[1] C. Bridges, *An Exposition of the Book of Ecclesiastes* (1960 reprint, pp. xiv–xv).
[2] *The Works of Wesley* (1898), vol. 4, p. 91.
[3] C. I. Scofield in his annotated edition of the AV.
[4] G. Bickell, *Der Prediger über den Wert des Dasiens* (1884) and *Koheleth's Untersuchung über den Wert des Dasiens* (1886).
[5] P. Haupt, *The Book of Ecclesiastes* (1905).
[6] D. C. Siegfried, *Prediger und Hoheslied* (1898).

Similarly, Barton saw the handiwork of a *hasîd* (devout man) and a *ḥokmâ* (wisdom) editor, as well as a final editor who added 1:2; 7:27 and 12:8. Podechard held similar views and asked whether there were not several final editors as well as the two main interpolators.[1]

In recent years there has been less acceptance of the extreme glossatorial theories of earlier days. Many modern scholars hold that Ecclesiastes is more or less a unity, but that it takes a negative stance *vis-à-vis* earlier Israelite orthodoxy. There may, it is held, be a few glosses but not as many as McNeile, Barton and Podechard maintained. Variations of thought may be only 'variations in temper and mood' (Gordis). K. Galling thinks it a series of entirely unrelated poems and that only 1:1–11 and 12:8–14 are later additions.[2] A. Bentzen considered it a heterodox unity.[3] For C. Kuhl only 3:17; 5:19; 8:5, 12, 13; 12:9–14 are insertional.[4] A. Weiser's list of glosses is: 2:26; 3:17; 5:19; 7:29; 8:5; 11:9; 12:7.[5] Eissfeldt's is: 2:26; 3:17; 7:18b, 26b; 8:5, 12b, 13a; 11:9b; 12:7b, 12–14.[6] Similar views are held by R. Kroeber[7] and R. H. Pfeiffer.[8] For J. A. Soggin it is a 'unified composition'.[9] A slight variant comes from R. Gordis who thinks some verses are satirical, others unannounced quotations, but that the book as a whole is a unity.

The view that it is a work of scepticism has been so dominant that F. L. Moriarty could write in 1960: 'That Qoheleth is sceptical goes without saying.'[10] Kuhl thought that the Preacher's God was not the God of Israel and that he was 'not the righteous God but a distant, hidden God, who introduces all the contradictions and tensions in life which Man has to suffer (3:1ff.) in order that Man shall fear Him (3:14)'. Thus Kuhl thought the Preacher had 'no personal relationship with his God', and that this explains his 'gloomy sub-Christian attitude which is also far removed from the piety of the Old Testament'.[11]

[1] For comparative tables of parts attributed to glossators, *cf. IB*, 5, p. 8.
[2] K. Galling, *Die Fünf Megilloth* (1940).
[3] A. Bentzen, *Introduction to the Old Testament*[2], vol. 2 (1952), p. 191.
[4] C. Kuhl, *The Old Testament, its Origins and Composition* (1961), p. 226.
[5] A. Weiser, *Introduction to the Old Testament* (1961), pp. 308–309.
[6] O. Eissfeldt, *The Old Testament – An Introduction* (1965), p. 499.
[7] R. Kroeber, *Der Prediger* (1963), p. 38.
[8] R. H. Pfeiffer, *Introduction to the Old Testament* (1948), p. 728.
[9] J. A. Soggin, *Introduction to the Old Testament* (1976), p. 399.
[10] F. L. Moriarty, *Introducing the Old Testament* (1960), p. 216.
[11] C. Kuhl, *The Old Testament, its Origin and Composition* (1961), pp. 264f.

Others have spoken of 'an amoral view of life on the basis of an amoral view of God'.[1]

Some, however, have thought that the Preacher's negativism proclaims indirectly the reality of God and of the life of faith. Thus Lauha thinks the purpose of Ecclesiastes is 'to disclose the hopelessness and untenability of the secularist concept of life and thereby to proclaim indirectly the living reality of God and the indispensability of a personal struggle of faith'.[2]

Two major questions therefore confront us: Does the book contain insertional material? Is it possible to find a purpose underlying the book which accounts for the phenomena of the text? To these we now turn.

VI. THE COMPOSITION OF ECCLESIASTES

Three basic reasons have been given for seeing insertional passages: the presence of editorial passages in 1:2; 7:27 and 12:8 where the Preacher is referred to in the third person; additional epilogues in 12:9f. and 12:11–14; and, most important, the contradictory elements within the book. 'Wise man' additions are felt to interrupt the sequence of thought. 'Pious additions' are said to vary in tone and sentiment from other sections and to come only when the Preacher approaches some heretical position.

Possible additions of the wise man are: 4:5, 9–12; 6:7; 7:1a, 5–12, 19; 8:1; 9:17–10:3; 10:8–14a, 15, 18f. Possible additions of the 'pious man' are 2:26a; 3:17; 7:18b, 26b, 29; 8:2b–3, 5–6a, 11–13; 11:9b; 12:1a, 13f. These are the passages whose authenticity is still in doubt despite the more conservative trend since Podechard's work in 1912. There are, however, major objections to theories of extensive insertional material.

The argument

It is very odd to imagine an 'editor' issuing a work with which he disagrees but adding extensive notes and an epilogue to compensate. Why should an orthodox writer reproduce a sceptical book at all, let alone add orthodox glosses to produce a noticeably mixed bag? It is quite conceivable that an editor sent out Ecclesiastes with a commendatory note, but it is scarcely likely that anyone would do this if he were unhappy with the content

---

[1] *Cf.* D. B. Macdonald, *The Hebrew Philosophical Genius: A Vindication* (1936), ch. 5.

[2] A. Lauha, *VTS*, 3, 1960, p. 191; *cf.* his commentary of 1978.

of the work. No wisdom document exists in two recensions with opposite theologies; it is doubtful if one ever did. It is possible to imagine an orthodox writer re-writing a dangerous work in order to counteract it; but if this were the case, he was singularly unsuccessful, for, *ex hypothesi*, he left the 'dangerous' views side by side with the orthodox ones. If we are capable of noticing this, surely he was.

To illustrate, we may consider in further detail 8:12f., where a sinner 'lives long' (according to v. 12), but does not 'prolong his days' (according to v. 13). Here, surely, is an internal contradiction. The sinner 'lives long', wrote an original Qoheleth; but 'he shall not prolong his days', wrote a pious scribe of later days. The argument is persuasive, yet has its difficulties. Why did the glossator leave the blatant contradiction, instead of amending clearly: 'Qoheleth says, Even though a sinner does evil and lives long...*But I say*, He shall not prolong...'? Or, since he was *ex hypothesi* revising Qoheleth's original, why not simply omit the offending remark? Every attempt to reconstruct the situation of an original writer plus correcting redactors results in redactors of great clumsiness or stupidity, adopting an editorial procedure which seems inherently unlikely.

It is surely more likely that juxtaposed contradictions (*e.g.* 8:12f.) are calculated to draw our attention to the viewpoint of faith in contrast to that of observation. As a point of empirical observation, there are those who do evil and live long. As a point of faith, the Preacher holds that this does not go on for ever: he shall not prolong his days. This is made more likely in that the introductory verbs are significantly different. The first aspect is introduced by the words 'I see...I have seen' (vv. 9f.); the viewpoint of faith is introduced by the words 'Yet I know'. Why should we postulate a clumsy self-contradicting scribe? Why may not the Preacher himself reply, from the viewpoint of faith, in v. 13 to a problem he has deliberately raised in v. 12 from the viewpoint of observation?

Underlying these considerations there is, however, a major question of method. The whole question of insertional material in biblical documents is tricky and arguments tend to be circular. The theory of unoriginal and intrusive insertions arises from the difficulty of expounding the fluctuating thought consistently and coherently. This difficulty tempts the interpreter to treat certain phrases as unoriginal, despite the absence of any *other* evidence of a variant.

But what if Ecclesiastes *can* be expounded coherently as it stands? In the one case an *a priori* conviction concerning exposition dictates the text; in the other, the text dictates the exposition. In the absence of any other evidence (and in this case there is none), surely the latter procedure must win our vote. If a coherent exposition can be given, is that not itself a positive indication that the text as we have it is original? (I leave aside the quite different question of the unintentional errors of copyists.)

The vocabulary

In Ecclesiastes there is the added difficulty that the vocabulary of the disputed sections is remarkably similar to that of the undisputed sections. Thus the disputed 2:26 contains *business*, which is a keyword in undisputed sections. In 3:17 *I said in my heart* and *there is a time* are recognizably the Preacher's style. In 4:9 *labour*, another key term, appears, and again in 6:7. *A good name is better than precious ointment* (7:1) and 7:5–12 are regarded as insertions; yet the 'better than' type of proverb is found throughout Ecclesiastes, while some expressions in 7:5–12 are decidedly reminiscent of the Preacher's language: *this also is vanity* (7:6), *an advantage to those who see the sun* (7:11), *advantage* (7:12).

In 7:7 *oppression* is discussed in terms similar to the undisputed 4:1–3. The 'fear of God' which is deleted from 7:18b; 8:12f. recalls 3:14 and 5:7 which are regarded as original. In 7:26 the autobiographical mode of presentation is distinctive of the Preacher (as is the pleonastic use of the first person singular pronoun in the Hebrew). *Before God* is also his term. 7:29 coheres well with the theology of Genesis 1 – 3 which underlies the book as a whole (*cf.* p. 46). In 7:11f., 19; 8:1; 9:18; 10:1, 10 allusions to wisdom are regarded as insertional. Although references to wisdom are too general to argue clearly one way or the other, yet it must be said that in the undisputed sections the Preacher is clearly a wise man himself, with a high regard for wisdom (1:13, 17; 2:9, 13; 7:23; 8:16; 9:15). *Wisdom gives strength* is said to be an insertion; *wisdom is better than strength* is not (7:19; 9:16). Despite the superficial difference, they really say the same thing in almost the same words. The oath of allegiance (8:2b) is deleted, yet it is clear from 5:9 that the Preacher discouraged rebellion.

In 8:5–6a *time* and *judgment* recall 3:16–22. 8:11–13 is deleted although it corresponds exactly to 3:16, 18–22 which is not. In addition the use of *ma*ᵃ*śeh*, the participle with pronoun style, the verb 'see' and *before God* all have parallels in indisputably authentic passages elsewhere. In 9:17 – 10:3 the 'better than' proverb recalls ch. 7. The disputed 9:17 recalls the undisputed 4:6, as 10:3 echoes 2:14. In 10:8–14a the term *advantage* (10f.) reflects the terminology of the bulk of the book. 10:14b is left in, presumably because it is manifestly the Preacher's language; yet the phrases on either side are said to be glosses (10:8–14a, 15). But 10:14b does not fit alongside 10:7 or 10:16. Where does it come from if it is not part of 10:14a and so proof of the Preacher's authorship? In 10:15, 19 the use of *labour*, the combination of *joy* and *laughter* (*cf.* 2:2 and the Hebrew of 10:19) are reminiscent of previous arguments. The *meat for enjoyment* (10:19) coheres with 2:25 and 3:22, yet is removed. The judgment in 11:9b and 12:14 recalls 3:16–22.

In short, the disputed sections are riddled with the Preacher's theology and vocabulary. If they are insertions, the glossators were skilful mimics indeed. Jastrow holds that an interpolator copied the Preacher's style. A simpler explanation is available! That Jones sees the interpolators using a 'different tone and sentiment', while Jastrow sees the interpolator copying the Preacher's style, indicates how subjective such judgments can be. There is in fact no reason for deleting verses from Ecclesiastes except an *a priori* conception of the Preacher's task that will not allow them to be there. They stand without textual dispute, and it is methodologically required that we approach the interpretation of Ecclesiastes in such a way as takes them into account.

The question as to whether the title (1:1) and epilogue (12:9–14) are the work of a writer distinct from the author of the bulk of the book have already been discussed under the question of authorship (see pp. 21–24).

The end of the matter

Whatever may be the textual history of Ecclesiastes, the present book is the only Ecclesiastes we have. Since its literary history is entirely hypothetical, the task of expounding any lost original is futile and impossible. Our Ecclesiastes is a work of literature in its own right and demands to be studied as such. The final stage of the text is all we have.[1]

---

[1] This approach has been recently urged by B. S. Childs, *Introduction to the Old Testament as Scripture* (1979), pp. 46–106. *Cf.* also G. T. Sheppard, 'The Epilogue to Qoheleth as Theological Commentary', *CBQ*, 39, 1977, pp. 182–189.

VII. THE PURPOSE OF ECCLESIASTES

A search for a convincing account of the purpose of Ecclesiastes must begin by accepting the textual integrity of the book as we have it. If the editorial revision were as substantial as is sometimes suggested, the question concerning its purpose would simply move on one stage to the question of the purpose of its editors. It is necessary, too, to accept the pessimistic strand within the book. For if critical orthodoxy has effectively deleted orthodox elements within Ecclesiastes, traditional orthodoxy has at times just as effectively ignored, played down or allegorized its pessimism. Neither squares with the book as we have it.

What, then, is the purpose of Ecclesiastes? It is an essay in apologetics. It defends the life of faith in a generous God by pointing to the grimness of the alternative.

Let us start with the heaven-earth dichotomy. The Preacher divides reality into two realms, one the dwelling-place of God, the other the dwelling-place of man. 'God is in heaven, and you upon earth' (5:2) is an underlying assumption throughout the text. Three expressions are used for the earthly side of this duality: 'under the sun', 'under heaven' and 'on earth'. The identity of 'under heaven' and 'under the sun' is clear from 1:13–14. There can be little doubt, although it is less easy to prove, that 'on earth' is a third synonym.

This style of language is know in other ancient works. Babylonian writings speak of the two realms. Marduk is 'lord of heaven and earth'.[1] To 'see the light of the sun' is to be alive, whereas the dead do not 'see the sun'.[2] Occasionally in Egyptian writings a similar antithesis is found. In *A Song of the Harper* 'over there' (the realm of the dead, the afterlife) is distinct from 'on earth'.[3] G. Ryckmans refers to similar formulae in South Arabian inscriptions.[4]

The expression 'under the sun' occurs also in an Elamite in-

[1] Lambert, p. 113, line 17; *cf.* also line 30.
[2] Lambert, p. 59, line 31 in the context of lines 29–36; Lambert, p. 201, reverse IV, line 2. *Cf.* also reference to 'heaven and earth' in *Nisaba and Wheat* (Lambert, p. 175, line 11)); in *Ludlul Bel Nemeqi* ('the earth is laid ... the heavens are laid out', Lambert, p. 59, line 37); and in *Address to a Prince* (Lambert, p. 115, line 42). The duality is also evident in *The Šamaš Hymn* (Lambert, pp. 126–138).
[3] *ANET*, p. 467.
[4] G. Ryckmans, 'Heaven and Earth in the South Arabian Inscriptions', *JSS*, 3, 1958, pp. 225–236, esp. p. 231.

scription.[1] Then in the late-fourth-century Phoenician inscription of Tabnith, king of Sidon, the phrase (Phoenician: *tht šmš*) has exactly the same form as in Ecclesiastes. The inscription refers to 'the living under the sun' (line 7), a contrast to the dead who are in a different realm altogether ('among the shades', line 8). Similar terminology is found in the late-fourth-century BC inscription of Eshmunnazar, king of Sidon (line 12).[2] Finally, the Greek writers Theognis and Euripides use similar expressions.[3]

Whether Ecclesiastes is directly borrowing from ancient terminology is uncertain, for such language is likely to emerge independently of actual contact with specific writings of surrounding cultures. What is clear is that the Preacher's style was easily comprehensible in the ancient world, and that he used the heaven-earth dichotomy for his own purposes. The Preacher's point is that what is to be seen with sheer pessimism 'under the sun' may be seen differently in the light of faith in the generosity of God: mankind gains nothing 'under the sun' (1:3); the 'earth' which is dominated by futility 'goes on for ever' (1:4); no new thing can take place 'under the sun' (1:9-11). As for the scope of the Preacher's researches, he sought out what was done 'under heaven' (1:13) and evaluated what resources could be found 'under the sun' (1:14). His quest for pleasure likewise found no hope of gain 'under the sun' (2:11); what is done 'under the sun' was grievous to him (2:17f.).

For much of the time the argument leaves God out of account. Then dramatically the Preacher introduces God and all changes. The 'under the sun' terminology falls into the background or lapses altogether (2:24-26; 11:1-12:14); instead he refers to the 'hand of God' (2:24), the joy of man (2:25; 3:12; 5:18, 20; 9:7; 11:7-9), and the generosity of God (2:26; 3:13; 5:19). Ecclesiastes is thus an exploration of the barrenness of life without a practical faith in God. Intermingled with its pessimism are invitations to a different outlook altogether, in which joy and purpose are found when God is seen to be 'there' and to be characterized supremely by generosity. On twelve occasions God is said to 'give'.[4] On seven occasions mankind is said to have a joyful 'portion' from God.[5]

[1] *Cf.* J. Friedrich, *Orientalia*, New Series, 18, 1948, pp. 28–29.
[2] *Cf.* H. Donner and W. Röllig, *Kanaanische und Aramäische Inschriften* (Band I, 1962), pp. 2–3 (texts 13 and 14).
[3] *Cf.* Plumptre, and Ranston, p. 25.
[4] Ec. 1:13; 2:26 (twice); 3:10, 11; 5:18, 19; 6:2; 8:15; 9:9; 12:7, 11.
[5] Ec. 2:10, 21; 3:22; 5:18, 19; 9:6, 9.

Another angle of approach is to consider the relationship between Ecclesiastes and Genesis 1 – 11. C. C. Forman has drawn attention to numerous points of contact. In the early chapters of Genesis the human race is excluded from the life-sustaining presence of God (Gn. 3:22–24) and the earth subjected to a curse (Gn. 3:17f.). Man is condemned to increased toil, his work no longer being part of an original bliss (Gn. 2:15) but a daily toil imposed upon him in judgment (Gn. 3:19). Death is his ultimate physical destiny (Gn. 3:19b). These themes are obvious links between Ecclesiastes and Genesis. Genesis speaks of the earth as cursed (3:17); the Preacher speaks of the kinks (*what is crooked*) and gaps (*what is lacking*) in life, irrevocable (1:15) because imposed by God (7:13). In Genesis man is an unstable combination of dust and breath (Gn. 2:7; 3:19); the Preacher says the same (Ec. 3:21; 12:7). Forman sees significance in the link between Abel (*hebel*) and 'vanity' (*hebel*). Whatever the original meaning of the name Abel, the Preacher uses its meaning 'vanity' as his theme-song. In Genesis man is originally upright, then falls; the Preacher highlights both the original righteousness (Ec. 7:29) and the calamitous results of a fall in man's life (Ec. 7:20). Forman points also to the similarity between Ecclesiastes 8:11; 9:3 and Genesis 6:5f.; Ecclesiastes 7:26ff. and the story of Eve's entangling the man (Gn. 3:6, 12); Ecclesiastes 9:9 and Genesis 2:18–25; the Preacher's preoccupation with man's ignorance and the story of man's exclusion from the tree of knowledge (Gn. 2:15ff.).[1] It would seem then that the Preacher is drawing on the themes of these Genesis chapters and is pressing home their implications.

A further notable feature of Ecclesiastes is its striking omissions. It makes no mention of Yahweh, the LORD, the name of the God of Israel's covenant faith. It scarcely refers to the law of God, the only possible reference being in 12:13. It scarcely refers to the nation of Israel (only in 1:12). Why these omissions? The answer seems to be that the Preacher's argument stands on its own feet and does not depend on Israel's covenant faith to be valid. He is appealing to universally observable facts, not restricted to Old Testament revelation. 'I have seen...I saw' are

---

[1] C. C. Forman, 'Koheleth's Use of Genesis', *JSS*, 5, 1960, pp. 256–263; this supplements an earlier article 'The Pessimism of Ecclesiastes', *JSS*, 3, 1958, pp. 336–343. W. Zimmerli also notes that 'There are many indications that Ecclesiastes knew even the combined text of Genesis 1 – 3' (*SJT*, 17, 1964, p. 155).

his characteristic phrases. The Phoenicians were allowed to bring stones to Israel's temple but not to dictate its over-all design. So pagan men can contribute building blocks. They can see, think, quarry basic facts. But do they discern the design behind the basic data of life? The Preacher points to an area of common ground, with very little reference to the distinctives of Israel's history and faith. He then presses the question: can the facts be lived with, except in the light of faith in a generous God?

It is striking, however, that when the Preacher refers to 'God', the Hebrew is rarely *ᵉlōhîm* (three instances only); it is normally *hāᵉlōhîm*, 'the God', the one who is known to him, the only one that he recognizes. The characteristic of God mentioned most often is his generosity. Thus the Preacher is dealing with a God who is known, and known to be generous.

The apostle Paul once preached a sermon to pagan philosophers in which, according to Acts 17, there was no mention of Scripture, of the nation of Israel, nor of the ministry of John the Baptist. The body of the sermon concerned 'you…your worship …the God who made the world…life and breath and everything…our being…the deity'. Only in his last sentence does he mention Jesus and then not by name, only as 'a man whom [God] has appointed'; his last phrase contains the only radically Christian element: 'the resurrection'.

The Preacher in his own pre-Christian way does something similar. Only at the end of his argument does he allude to God's commandments. He begins not by pressing the need of obedience, but much further back, at the point where everyone finds himself, here in this world, confronted by certain observable realities. Nor does the Preacher lead us all the way to Messianic faith. His work is not full-orbed evangelism; it is the opening sentences of an evangelistic message, leading to faith along a pathway of conviction of need. He asks everyman, starting with the same building material, whether he has learnt to cope with *this* life as it really is.

A subsidiary implication of the Preacher's argument is the limit set to wisdom. As he points to the futility of all human life 'under the sun', wisdom too is shown to be inadequate to help. Wisdom given by God, acted out in the presence of God, is allowed; autonomous, self-sufficient wisdom as a remedy to man's plight 'under the sun' is disallowed. Thus there is much truth in Zimmerli's statement that Ecclesiastes is the 'frontier-guard, who forbids wisdom to cross the frontier towards a comprehensive art of life'.[1]

Yet the Preacher's purpose is bigger than that. He sets a limit not only to wisdom but to *all* human resources. He is the frontier-guard against *any* form of self-reliance. The fear of God which he recommends (3:14; 5:7; 8:12; 12:13) is not only the beginning of wisdom; it is also the beginning of joy, of contentment and of an energetic and purposeful life.

The Preacher wishes to deliver us from a rosy-coloured, self-confident godless life, with its inevitable cynicism and bitterness, and from trusting in wisdom, pleasure, wealth, and human justice or integrity. He wishes to drive us to see that God is there, that he is good and generous, and that only such an outlook makes life coherent and fulfilling.

VIII. THE STRUCTURE AND ANALYSIS OF ECCLESIASTES

Some commentators declare that Ecclesiastes has no structure at all. R. E. Murphy once wrote: 'No one will ever succeed in giving a satisfactory outline of the contents of the book. Any schematic outline superimposes upon the meditation of Coheleth a framework that he certainly never had in mind.'[2] Many have, therefore, seen the Preacher's work as a string of unrelated meditations. A. G. Wright lists twenty-three commentators who virtually abandon the task of seeking coherence in the book (among them Delitzsch, Barton, Galling, Hertzberg, Scott and Barucq).[3] This list could easily be enlarged.

Others have tried to find progression of thought. Wright mentions Bea, Ginsberg, Zöckler, Podechard, Buzy and others,[4] and refers to the objective criteria that a few (Ginsberg, Hitzig *et al.*) tried to find.[5] More recently Lys and Loader[6] have also presented interpretations in which the Preacher's work holds together.

---

[1] W. Zimmerli, 'The Place and Limit of the Wisdom in the Framework of the Old Testament Theology', *SJT*, 17, 1964, pp. 146–158, esp. p. 158.

[2] *Cf.* R. E. Murphy, 'The Pensées of Coheleth', *CBQ*, 17, 1958, pp. 184–194.

[3] *Cf.* A. G. Wright, 'The Riddle of the Sphinx: The Structure of the Book of Qoheleth', *CBQ*, 30, 1968, p. 313.

[4] *Cf.* A. G. Wright, *art. cit.*, p. 314, for references.

[5] *Ibid.*, pp. 315–316.

[6] J. A. Loader, *Polar Structures in the Book of Qohelet* (1979). It is noteworthy that Loader does not wish his view of polar structures to be confused with the formal structure of the literary units of the book (p. 1).

Wright's own position is that the eightfold repetition in 1:12 – 6:9 of 'vanity and a chase after wind' marks eight meaningful units which make up the first major section of the book. A series of similar statements, four allusions to our inability to find sense in the world, and six references to our ignorance, identifies a second major section (6:10 – 11:6). A title (1:1), two poems (1:2–11; 11:7 – 12:8) and an epilogue (12:9–14) complete the book. In a later article, Wright suggests that his thesis is confirmed by numerical patterns within Ecclesiastes.[1]

In the present writer's opinion, attempts to find a detailed and intricate structure in Ecclesiastes have not been successful. The recurrence of the phrase 'vanity and a striving after wind' or references to 'finding out' or 'not knowing' indicate dominant interests in the Preacher's wisdom. It is doubtful whether Wright is correct in thinking these are intended to be precise dividing-lines and indications of formal structure. At several points (*e.g.* 1:15; 2:17; 7:24; 8:17) a division seems unsuitable. Does a new sub-section really start after 1:17, or in 7:25? Other attempts at finding detailed structures (*e.g.* that of H. L. Ginsberg[2]) involve a large number of postulated disgressions and present no objective criteria for the analysis.

However, there are indications of a sense of purpose and progress within Ecclesiastes. Although it cannot be argued that any objective structure was demonstrably present in the mind of the writer or his editor, yet it is helpful to point out such connected passages and progressions of thought as can be discerned. There is a sense in which any analysis of any book of the Bible is an imposition. The biblical writers did not use headings and sub-headings, let alone chapters and verses. They present their material with no modern aids. Presumably, however, they knew what they wanted to say, and, evidently, did not write in a totally random manner. By all means let us seek to illumine the main shape of their argument, but let us constantly beware of the danger of imposing on any book a rigid pattern that would amaze its author. Content is prior to form, and enthusiasm may override structure.

---

[1] A. G. Wright, 'The Riddle of the Sphinx Revisited: Numerical Patterns in the Book of Qoheleth', *CBQ*, 42, 1980, pp. 38–51. The summary here hardly does justice to Wright's articles, which should be consulted.

[2] *Cf.* H. L. Ginsberg, 'The Structure and Contents of the Book of Koheleth', *WIANE*, pp. 138–149.

ECCLESIASTES

The content of Ecclesiastes may be set out as follows with the minimum attempt to discern major sections of thought.

1. Title (1:1)
2. The failure of secularism (1:2–11)
3. The failure of wisdom (1:12–18)
4. The failure of pleasure-seeking (2:1–11)
5. Life's ultimate certainty (2:12–23)
6. The life of faith (2:24–26)
7. The providence of God (3:1–15)
8. The judgment of God (3:16–22)
9. Oppression without comfort (4:1–3)
10. Lonesome rivalry and its alternatives (4:4–6)
11. A man without a family (4:7–8)
12. The blessings of companionship (4:9–12)
13. Isolation breeding folly (4:13–16)
14. The approach to God (5:1–7)
15. The poor under oppressive bureaucracy (5:8–9)
16. Money and its drawbacks (5:10–12)
17. Wealth – loved and lost (5:13–17)
18. Remedy recalled (5:18–20)
19. Wealth and its insecurity (6:1–6)
20. Insatiable longing (6:7–9)
21. An impasse (6:10–12)
22. Instruction from suffering (7:1–6)
23. Four dangers (7:7–10)
24. The need of wisdom (7:11–12)
25. Life under the hand of God (7:13–14)
26. Dangers along the way (7:15–18)
27. The need of wisdom (7:19–22)
28. The inaccessibility of wisdom (7:23–24)
29. The sinfulness of man (7:25–29)
30. Who is really wise? (8:1)
31. Royal authority (8:2–8)
32. Life's injustices (8:9–11)
33. The life of faith (8:12–13)
34. Again: life's injustices (8:14)
35. Again: the life of faith (8:15)
36. The enigma of life (8:16 – 9:1)
37. 'The sting of death' (9:2–3)
38. Where there's life, there's hope (9:4–6)
39. The remedy of faith (9:7–10)

There is a lot to be said for leaving it at this. Yet as one studies Ecclesiastes it appears that there is more to be said. It is argued in the following commentary that there are explicit, objective indications of progression of thought in the Preacher's mind. They include the following: (i) The obvious fact that 1:1 is a title. (ii) An observable trend in argument in 1:2 – 2:23. (iii) An observable turn in the argument at 2:24 with several objective differences between what follows and what precedes. (iv) A coherence of subject-matter in 4:1–16; 5:8 – 6:12; 9:11 – 10:20, and to a lesser extent in 7:1 – 8:1 and 8:2 – 9:10. (v) The observable rise of sustained exhortation in 11:1 – 12:8. (vi) The obvious fact that 12:9–14 is an appendage either by the writer or by an editor.

None of these considerations is subjective; all are there in the text. It may be concluded, therefore, that as the Preacher compiled his proverbs, sayings and arguments, in his mind ran a trend of thought that may be represented as follows overleaf:

ECCLESIASTES

This leaves the following loose ends which warn us not to assume that all of this was too rigidly in the Preacher's mind as he wrote: (i) 5:1–7 tags on to the end of 4:1–16 or introduces 5:8 – 6:12) but is not closely linked to either. One may speculate about a sequence of thought (as is attempted in the commentary); but no explicit link is found in the text. (ii) Although 3:16–22 coheres well with 2:24 – 3:15, it also leads into the problem of suffering in 4:1–3 (which has its own links in turn with 4:4–16). (iii) There is only a loose coherence in the minor units of 7:1 – 8:1 and 8:2 – 9:10.

COMMENTARY

I. Pessimism: its problems and its remedy (1:1 – 3:22)

IN the opening chapters the thought passes from exposing a problem (1:2 – 2:23) to presenting a basic outline of its solution (2:24 – 3:22). The problem is that of life itself. If viewed without reference to God ('under the sun'), the world in which we find ourselves is a chaos without meaning or progress (1:2–11); neither wisdom (1:12–18) nor pleasure (2:1–11) will enable us to live contentedly. Over both hangs a dark shadow: the inevitability of death (2:12–23). Thus the Preacher lays the foundation for commending a God-centred view of life by presenting a critique of all forms of secularism, whether theoretical ('There is no God'; cf. Ps.14:1) or pragmatic ('I don't care about God'). To any who maintain a viewpoint other than the faith of Israel he asks in effect: Do you realize what follows from your view of life?

The Preacher himself sees life as more than the sum of what is seen 'under the sun'; the problems of life are given us by God (cf. 1:13). The pessimistic viewpoint, however, is unaccompanied by any practical faith in a God who may be trusted. With this earth-bound horizon it despairs of finding meaning or satisfaction in life. The Preacher will have his readers see the grimness of the pessimist viewpoint before he points to a life that derives from God himself (2:24 – 3:22).

A. TITLE (1:1)

1. *Son of David, king in Jerusalem* refers to Solomon, but the artificial name 'Mr Preacher' (for so it might be paraphrased) shows that the writer is not seriously claiming to be Solomon. The book is a write-up of Solomon's story; later we shall be told that the originator of the material was a careful writer, a wise man, a collector of proverbs (12:9–12).[1]

---

[1] See Introduction, pp. 21–24 for fuller detail.

B. THE PESSIMIST'S PROBLEMS (1:2 – 2:23)

i. The failure of secularism (1:2–11). The Preacher under-mines confidence in the secular view of life by inviting his readers to face some basic facts: the futility of life (v.2), its consequences for man (3), the impossibility of getting rid of the earthly realm which embodies the problem (4), and the impli-cations all this has for man's view of nature (5–7) and history (8–11). It is a practical, not necessarily a full-blown intellectual, secularism that is in view. For there is a secularism of indifference or timidity, as well as of philosophy. Equally it is not to be thought that opinions are being presented as 'merely' the secular viewpoint, and not as in fact true. For the Preacher these *are* facts, but they are not the whole truth. He can describe his own life as a 'vain life' (7:15), but his outlook includes more than the earthly realm.

2. *Vanity of vanities* is a Hebrew superlative: 'Utter vanity!' *Vanity* (*hebel*) includes (i) brevity and unsubstantiality, *emptiness* (NEB), spelt out in Job 7 where the 'vanity' (v.16, Heb.) of man's life is a 'breath' (v.7), an evaporating cloud (v.9), soon to be ended (v.8) and return no more (vv.9f.); (ii) unreliability, frailty, found also in Psalm 62 where God, a 'Rock' and a 'high tower' (v.6), is compared with man who is 'vanity' (v.9), a 'leaning wall' and a 'tottering fence' (v.3); (iii) futility, as in Job 9:29 (Heb.), where 'in vanity' means 'to no effect'; (iv) deceit (*cf.* Je. 16:19; Zc. 10:2).[1] Ecclesiastes includes each of these emphases. All is untrustworthy, unsubstantial; no endeavour will in itself bring permanent satisfaction; the greatest joys are fleeting. Between 1:2 and 12:8 the Preacher will echo this key statement about thirty times, showing that his book is in fact its exposition. *Vanity* characterizes all human activity (1:14; 2:11): joy (2:1) and frustration (4:4, 7–8; 5:10) alike, life (2:17; 6:12; 9:9), youth (11:10) and death (3:19; 11:8), the destinies of wise and foolish (2:15, 19), diligent and idle (2:21, 23, 26).

All is literally 'the whole'. All earthly experience, seen as a

---

[1] Less central in the usage of *hebel* are ideas of 'incomprehensibility' (*cf.* NIV; W. E. Staples, 'The "Vanity" of Ecclesiastes', *JNES*, 2, 1943, pp. 95–104), 'zero' (H. L. Ginsberg, *WIANE*, p. 138) or 'something very close to "irony" and "ironic"' which is 'used to point out incongruities' (E. M. Good, *Irony in the Old Testament* (1965), p. 182, followed closely by T. Polk, 'The Wisdom of Irony', *Studia Biblica et Theologica*, 6, 1976, pp. 3–17). Other views are mentioned by Lys (p. 89).

unit, is 'subject to vanity' (*cf.* Rom. 8:20). The same expression occurs in the Hebrew of 1:14; 2:11, 17; 3:1, 19; 12:8. A qualification is found in v.3 ('under the sun'), repeated in 1:14; 2:11, 17; and, with variation, 3:1. It is only to one seeking satisfaction in disregard of God that the Preacher's message stops at 'All is vanity'. For any who adopt his total world-view he has a note of encouragement. When a perspective of faith is introduced 'All is vanity' is still true, but it is not the whole picture; 'under the sun' it is the whole truth. When, in 2:24 – 3:22 and intermittently thereafter, new factors are brought in (the generosity of God, divine providence, divine judgment), the 'vanity' of life is not obliterated or forgotten; but the new factors transform the perspective and turn pessimism into faith. This prefigures the New Testament perspective in which the believer is 'outwardly …wasting away' (2 Cor. 4:16), is 'subjected to vanity' and 'groans' with creation 'right up to the present time' (Rom. 8:20–22). Yet he 'knows' what is happening (Rom. 8:22), 'gazes' at a different perspective (2 Cor. 4:18), 'waits' for something different (Rom. 8:25). The new perspective does not cancel out the old; the believer is living in an overlap. But the new perspective revolutionizes his outlook.

3. This verse explains the consequences of earthly futility for mankind himself. *Gain* (*yiṭrôn*) is a commercial term; life 'pays no dividends' (Jones). If the earthly realm is subject to vanity, there is no hope of finding ultimate gain or satisfaction from its resources alone. *Labour* (*ʿāmāl*) may denote physical toil (Ps. 127:1) or mental anguish (Ps. 25:18). In Ecclesiastes the emphasis is generally on the actual labour of human endeavours (especially in 2:10f., 18–23), but the mental-emotional aspects of human *labour* must also be borne in mind here. This accords with the use of *ʿāmāl* elsewhere: Joseph's 'anguish' of mind (Gn. 41:51), the 'misery' from which Israel was delivered (Nu. 23:21, NIV), Job's 'trouble' (Jb. 3:10).[1] If our view of life goes no further than 'under the sun', all our endeavours will have an undertone of misery.

In the Old Testament *under the sun* occurs only in Ecclesiastes (1:3, 9, 14; 2:11, 17, 18, 19, 20, 22; 3:16; 4:1, 3, 7, 15; 5:13, 18; 6:1, 5, 12; 8:9, 15 (twice), 17; 9:3, 6, 9 (twice), 11, 13; 10:5). It has links

---

[1] C. S. Knopf includes 'opaqueness' in its meaning ('The Optimism of Koheleth', *JBL*, 49, 1930, pp. 195–199) but this is doubtful, C. C. Forman ('Koheleth's Use of Genesis', *JSS*, 5, 1956, p. 262) and Lys (p. 100) point to the background in Genesis 3.

with other ancient writings, for it occurs in Phoenician, Elamite and Greek writings.[1] *Vanity* characterizes man and the realm he occupies and dominates. If his resources are entirely this-worldly, 'No profit' is the motto over all he does. There is another realm altogether, the Preacher will contend later (5:2), when he will speak of God who may be approached and worshipped (5:1–7). Meanwhile the abyss of pessimism has to be explored.

4. Mankind's problem is further aggravated by the contrast between the brevity of life and the apparent permanence of the earthly realm (*cf.* Ps. 90:4f., where man is as effective as a midnight watch, as energetic as sleep, as enduring as grass). Thus the inherent vanity of the earthly realm gives no hope of change. *Goes…comes…remains* represent Hebrew participles and imply continuity of action, 'is continually going…coming… remaining'. *For ever* means that 'under the sun' there is no conceivable end to the problem of earthly futility.

5–7. These verses amplify vv.2–4 in terms of creation. Though a hubbub of activity, it is devoid of progress. There is no gain for man in his toil; similarly there is no gain for creation in her toil. Three examples are given: the repetitious cycles of the sun, like a runner on a circular track; the wind blowing round its circuits to no apparent purpose; the waters gushing into the seas without ever finding their task accomplished.

For Old Testament orthodoxy, creation rings with the praises of the LORD. Creation is his. Clouds, storms, thunder, lightning, all are within his control. The fertility of men, animals and plants are his to withhold or to give. He sets the bounds to the seas, orders summer and winter, makes the sun rule the day, the moon the night, and brings out the stars by number.[2] But, says the Preacher, take away its God, and creation no longer reflects his glory; it illustrates the weariness of mankind. When Adam fell, creation fell (Gn. 3:17–19). If man is weary, creation is weary with him. If our outlook is merely 'under the sun', no doxology can arise to one who is 'in heaven' (Ec. 5:2). The prophets' hope of mankind redeemed and an earthly paradise regained (Is. 11:6–9; 65:17–25) cannot stand on secular premises.

Hastens (RSV) translates a verb meaning 'to gasp, pant, sniff'.

---

[1] See Introduction, pp. 17–21, for references, and the significance of the phrase for the interpretation of Ecclesiastes.

[2] See further L. Koehler, *Old Testament Theology* (1957), pp. 26–29, 85–92; H. H. Rowley, *The Faith of Israel* (1956), pp. 25–27; J. L. McKenzie, 'God and Nature in the Old Testament', *CBQ*, 14, 1952, pp. 18–39, 124–145.

It depicts the sun as weary, like 'a runner breathing heavily in the race'.[1] The repeated participles of v.6, *going...turning... turning...going*, themselves give a feeling of monotony. In v.7, RSV *to the place where the streams flow* is correct. The thought is not that rivers return to their source (AV, NIV; NEB emends the text with the same ideas as a result), rather that rivers perpetually flow but make no progress in filling the sea.

8. The argument is taken a step further. Despite the fact that creation is active to the point of inexpressible exhaustion, it is incapable of providing secular man with any lasting satisfaction. *Full of weariness* is best taken passively ('wearied') rather than actively, following its clear meaning in its other occurrences (Dt. 25:18; 2 Sa. 17:2). *All things* may be translated 'All words', which would emphasize that the dissatisfaction of man is beyond words (*cf.* NAB *All speech is laboured*). That thought comes in the next phrase, but here the common translation carries the argument forward more clearly.

This 'under the sun' viewpoint again contrasts with that of the Old Covenant believer, who loved creation and saw in it the majesty of God's name,[2] looked with admiration at the skies,[3] pondered the lessons taught by animals, wind, grass and trees,[4] and sang to the glory of God because of what he saw and heard.[5] He saw nature sing for joy,[6] and knew that God's control of creation was part of his redemption at the time of the exodus.[7] Taking their cue from Solomon,[8] the wise men also gloried in creation and used its object-lessons for their own purposes.[9] The Preacher's point is that all this is lost in an 'under the sun' viewpoint; all that is left is nature in a state of exhaustion.

[1] N. H. Snaith, *Distinctive Ideas of the Old Testament* (1944), p. 145. P. Joüon ('Notes philologiques sur le texte Hébreu d'Ecclésiaste', *Bib*, 11, 1930, p. 419) contends that the text is suspect, but to understand it as above makes good sense in context.
[2] Pss. 8:1, 9; 19:1; 89:9–12; 96:11–12.
[3] Pss. 8:3; 19:1, 4–6.
[4] Pss. 32:9; 34:10; 35:5; 37:2, 35; 42:1; 50:10–11; 55:6–7; 58:4–8; 59:6; 74:12–17; 77:16–19; 84:3; 93:3–4; 102:4, 6–7.
[5] Pss. 8; 19; 29; 65; 104.
[6] Ps. 65:12–13.   [7] Ps. 78.
[8] 1 Ki. 4:33. No good reason exists to doubt that Solomon gave considerable impetus to wisdom literature in Israel, although its origins are earlier and international. See Introduction, pp. 28–36.
[9] Jb. 28:7–8; 39:1–30; 41:1–34; Pr. 1:27; 5:19; 6:5–8; 7:22–23; 25:13; 27:8; 28:1, 15; 30:15, 19, 31.

The verb *has...its fill* (*šābaʿ*) normally refers to the 'satisfying' of physical hunger (*e.g.* Ex. 16:8, 12), but here refers to being emotionally and psychologically *satisfied* (RSV).

9–10. These verses amplify vv.2–4 in terms of hope. If God is left aside, and life viewed 'under the sun', there can be nothing new; history is a closed circuit. Neither circumstances (*what has been*) nor human endeavours (*what has been done*) can change. This too contrasts with Israelite orthodoxy. The Hebrew believed history was controlled by God. 'Shall calamity befall a city and the LORD has not done it?' (Am. 3:6). The severe trials that befell Joseph and Job were attributed to God (Gn. 50:20; Jb. 42:2). Nebuchadrezzar was God's servant (Je. 25:9), Cyrus his anointed (Is. 45:1). Redemption consists of acts of God in history (*cf.* Ps. 106). Revelation involves authorized interpreters to predict God's acts before they happen, and to expound them after. History is travelling to a goal, the Day of the LORD, when he will complete his purpose, redeem his people and judge his enemies.[1]

Again, the Preacher's point is that this cannot be viewed secularly. Consider life 'under the sun' and the concept of God's ruling from heaven no longer holds good. No-one can appeal to God to 'look down' and intervene (Is. 63:15). There can be no redemption, for no new factor can be introduced. The heavenly realm is the source of what is really new, the psalmist's 'new song' (Ps. 96:1) and the prophet's 'new thing' (Is. 43:19).

In v.10 an objection is anticipated: what about that which is observably new? The answer is, it is illusory. The similarity to Greek, especially Stoic, thinking has often been pointed out.

---

[1] B. Albrektson's *History and the Gods* (1967) argues persuasively that this view of history and nature was not unique to Israel (although it is more central in Old Testament thinking) and that (contrary to earlier views) the gods of surrounding nations were thought of as lords of both nature and history (rather than lords of nature but not of history). Albrektson also argues that the contrast between revelation in history and revelation through word is a needless antithesis. Both in Israelite and in non-Israelite thought bare events are mute and do not reveal the deity's reasons for the event. 'The revelation in words...plays an important role' (pp. 117, 119). This is a more reliable reading of Old Testament and ancient non-Israelite thought than to posit a needless contrast between revelation through history and revelation through inspired word (*cf.* J. Baillie, *The Idea of Revelation in Recent Thought* (1956), pp. 62ff.). However, Albrektson has not explained why the Hebrews produced historiography on a high level unknown elsewhere in the ancient world (*cf.* W. G. Lambert's comments in *Orientalia*, 39, 1970, pp. 170–177). For a succinct and penetrating survey of different philosophies of history, see David Bebbington, *Patterns in History* (1979).

Von Rad thinks that the Preacher capitulated to secular philosophy at this point.[1] But the Preacher's identification with an earthbound horizon is only part of his exposition; the vertical perspective is yet to come.

11. This stage of the argument closes by considering mankind's approach to life in the light of the pessimistic evaluation of history in vv.9f. Nihilism not only dominates his outlook, it also works itself out in life. Past events are forgotten; future events will be forgotten. Here *remembrance*, deriving from the verb 'remember', means 'remembering and acting accordingly', a well-attested usage. Nehemiah's prayer 'Remember me for good' (Ne. 13:31) pleads that God's actions may arise out of his past promises (*cf.* Gn. 40:14; Ex. 20:8).[2]

Commentators have debated whether the translation should read 'former people' (NIV, Lys and others) or *former things* (RSV). The first has parallels in 2:16 and 9:15, but here vv.9f. are dealing with history more generally. Aalders (following Thilo) is surely right in thinking the antithesis needless. In the light of the word *ages* in v.10, he wishes to translate 'former times' and to include both people and circumstances.[3]

The orthodox Israelite lived in the light of former events (Dt. 5:15; 8:2; Ps. 77:11). Later the Preacher will invite us to 'remember' our Creator (12:1), live accordingly, and 'keep in mind' what lies ahead (11:8). On secular premises that is all pointless. 'Under the sun' the past, the present and the future offer no meaning, no guide-lines. This is the logical outworking of vv.2–10, the downward spiral of despair. Secular man will confirm the maxim, 'He who does not learn from history is destined to repeat it.'[4]

ii. The failure of wisdom to satisfy secular life (1:12–18).

After the pessimism of 1:2–11, the following sections shut off all escape routes. Will a man seek refuge in wisdom? It will only frustrate its secular devotees (1:12–18). Will he then hide from life's problems by squeezing the juice out of its pleasures? The juice turns sour (2:1–11). Does he live in a man-centred world

---

[1] G. von Rad, *Old Testament Theology*, vol. 1 (1962), p. 455.

[2] *Cf.* B. S. Childs, *Memory and Tradition in Israel* (1962), pp. 21f.

[3] The matter cannot be settled by appeal to the principle that the English neuter is expressed by the Hebrew feminine. There is the possibility of exceptions to the rule and the terms are strictly adjectives and may (as Aalders notes) be not neuter but masculine alluding to the masculine *ages* in v.10.

[4] JB *next year* is without warrant in the Hebrew.

devoid of absolutes? There is one certainty: death (2:12–23). Elsewhere the Preacher portrays wisdom as one of life's blessings, but in 1:12–18 the argument is different. Wisdom has value, but it will fail to solve the problem of life.

12. The kingly position adopted in 1:1 is reaffirmed as a major step forward in the argument is taken. Solomon, of all men, had the resources to make the investigations documented; we are exploring his story. The artificial name signals the literary device.[1]

13. The Preacher *set his heart, i.e.* was sincere and earnest; *heart* (RSV *mind*), as opposed to the 'outward appearance' (1 Sa. 16:7), denotes the inner life, the centre of all mental, emotional and spiritual capacities. His thoroughness is also indicated by *study...explore* (NIV; RSV *seek...search out*). The first means to 'search deeply' into something, the latter 'to search thoroughly over the widespread'; together they convey exhaustive study. *All that is done under heaven* shows that the total resources of a limited world-view are the object of study; the vertical aspect is not yet in view.

Three conclusions follow. First, 'God has appointed an unhappy task for the sons of men to do'. The verb 'give' sometimes has the force of 'appoint' (*e.g.* Je. 1:5). People may live secularly in the earthly realm, but the problems they meet are ordained by the God who occupies the heavenly realm. Mankind cannot be indifferent to or detached from the futility which besets him; it is an 'inescapable fact of one's humanity' (Rylaarsdam). *Business* (RSV; Heb. *'inyan;* NIV *burden*), denoting mankind's restlessness and vigour in the quest for meaning, derives from *'ānāh*, 'to engage in something', 'to be active in doing something'. It points to the sense of compulsion behind the quest. Mankind thinks and plans. This he can scarcely avoid, for he wants to understand where his life is going. This is the burden which, by God's decree, every man bears: the problem of life is no optional hobby.

> The wheels of life
> Stand never idle, but go always round.[2]

14. The second conclusion is that mankind is necessarily frustrated. He desires a sense of gain in life (1:3), of satisfaction

---

[1] See Introduction, pp. 21–24, for fuller detail.
[2] Matthew Arnold, 'Sonnet to the Duke of Wellington'.

in the world around him (1:8) and in the progress of history (1:9–11), but this eludes him.

Under the sun limits the statement to the seen world, interpreted in terms of itself. The immediate context is preoccupation with wisdom. To all practical purposes this man's life excludes God. He is faced with problems which he finds insoluble, with history which is repetitive and without hope. The immediate corollary of God's ordained task for him therefore is frustration. Delitzsch wishes to limit *everything that is done* to human deeds, but a review of the twenty-one instances of the term in Ecclesiastes shows that it includes all the events of the world, the deeds of God and men.

The meaning of *striving after wind* (RSV; AV *vexation of spirit*) is difficult to determine. The phrase (r^e '$\hat{u}\underline{t}$ $r\hat{u}^a\underline{h}$) has been derived from 'to break' (r'' or rss), giving the translation 'affliction of spirit'; from 'to strive' ($r'h$), giving 'striving for the wind'; from 'to feed' ($r'h$), hence 'feeding on wind'; from 'to desire' ($r'h$), which yields 'desiring the wind'. It has been linked with Aramaic and Phoenician cognates. The Hebrew $r\hat{u}^a\underline{h}$ may mean 'spirit' or 'wind'. The context equally suits two notions: frustration by the insoluble (*vexation of spirit*), or ambition for the unattainable (*striving after wind*). The latter is almost certainly the meaning here (and in 1:17; 2:11, 17, 26; 4:4, 6, 16; 6:9), for it has parallels in the Old Testament imagery of wind and since in 5:16 'toil for the wind' cannot easily mean 'toil for the spirit'.

15. The third conclusion explains why the 'under the sun' thinker is so frustrated. It is because there are twists (*what is crooked*) and gaps (*what is lacking*) in all thinking. No matter how the thinker ponders, he cannot straighten out life's anomalies, nor reduce all he sees to a neat system. Thus he reiterates the age-old problem of the wise men of the ancient Near East: awareness of finitude and inability to discover unaided the truth about life. Frustration and perplexity surround the philosopher. His wisdom may help in some things, but it cannot solve the fundamental problem of life.[1]

The Hebrew text should be translated 'cannot become straight'. A small emendation (*liṯqōn* to *l* tuqqan*)[2] would lead to 'cannot be made straight' (AV, RSV).

16–18. The Preacher explains the anguish of the secular philosopher, even though he be a Solomon-back-from-the-dead

---

[1] For parallels in Babylonian and Egyptian wisdom, *cf.* J. C. Rylaarsdam, *Revelation in Jewish Wisdom Literature* (1946), pp. 15–16.

[2] *Cf.* G. R. Driver, *VT*, 4, 1954, p. 225.

(v.16 echoes 1 Ki. 10:7).[1] *Has had great experience* is literally 'has seen'. In Ecclesiastes 'to see' is sometimes used literally (1:8; 5:11; 12:3); sometimes it means 'conclude, realize' (2:3; 3:18, *etc.*); sometimes 'to observe, reflect, consider' (1:14; 2:12; *etc.*), and sometimes, as here, 'to enjoy, experience' (1:16; 2:1, *etc.*). With NAB and Berkeley it is best in v.17 to translate *to know wisdom and knowledge, madness and folly*.[2] This raises the question of the apparently arbitrary introduction of *madness and folly*. The point is probably that, as the Preacher thought about wisdom and knowledge, he kept one eye on the alternatives. Thus the next section on pleasure-seeking is anticipated. The attempt to solve the problem of life by wisdom in fact only enlarged the problem (v.18). So long as wisdom is restricted to the realm 'under the sun', it sees the throbbing tumult of creation, life scurrying round its ever-repetitive circuits, and nothing more. 'The more you understand, the more you ache' (Moffatt).

iii. The failure of pleasure-seeking to satisfy secular life (2:1–11).
Having outlined the problem of futility and shown that wisdom cannot unravel the enigma, the Preacher now argues that pleasure-seeking cannot quench man's spiritual thirst. We are told first of his resolve (1a) and his conclusions (1b–2). Then follows a detailed account of his endeavours (3–8), the height of splendour and self-indulgence he attained (9f.) and his conclusions reiterated (11).

1a. Here *said* indicates a decision (*cf.* 7:23). The Preacher addresses himself in a style similar to the Egyptian *Man Who Was Tired With Life* ('I opened my mouth to my soul…').[3] *Come now* is 'used for incitement' (Ginsburg, illustrating from Nu. 22:6; Jdg. 19:11). NIV *I will test you with pleasure* translates accurately; the Hebrew spelling is uncommon but has parallels in the Qumran scrolls. The Preacher is not testing pleasure so much as himself. *I will plunge* (NEB) apparently takes the verb as meaning 'I will pour myself out in' (from *nāsak*, instead of MT *nāsāh*), but is less probable.

1b-2. Characteristically the conclusion comes before the substantiation. Hedonism shares in the *vanity* of all earthly

---

[1] *Cf.* pp. 21-24.
[2] AV and RSV follow the MT and treat *uᵉdaʿaṭ* as a construct governing *hōlēlûṭ wᵉsiḵlûṭ*. NAB and Berkeley ignore the Hebrew accents but produce a more balanced sentence. The ancient versions understood the passage in a similar way (*cf.* Aalders).
[3] *Cf.* R. O. Faulkner, *JEA*, 42, 1956, p. 21.

phenomena. Two items are specified: *laughter* (*śᵉḥôq*) and *mirth* (*śimḥâ*). The former is superficial gaiety, used of the 'fun' of a game (Pr. 10:23) or a party (Ec. 10:19), or the 'derision' which Jeremiah suffered (Je. 20:7). Though the distinction cannot always be sharply drawn, *śimḥâ* is thoughtful pleasure, the joy of religious festivals (Nu. 10:10; Jdg. 16:23), gratitude in serving the LORD (Dt. 28:47), or the proclamation of a king (1 Ki. 1:40). The two kinds of joy receive appropriate verdicts. The first, *laughter*, is *mad*. The verbal root (*hll*) is associated with loss of judgment (*cf.* Jb. 12:17; Ec. 7:7); rather than face life as it is, the merry-maker drowns the hard facts in a sea of frivolity. As for weightier *pleasure* (*śimḥâ*), the Preacher simply asks: What does it achieve? Does it produce a fundamental change, any answers, any satisfaction? The implication of the rhetorical question is obvious: all pleasures, highbrow and lowbrow alike, fail to meet the needs of the man whose horizon remains 'under the sun'.

3. The Preacher now goes into detail. His quest was persistent (*till I might see*), confined to a limited area (*under heaven*), deliberate and serious (for his heart *acts in wisdom*).[1] The last clause, *till I might see...* probably attaches to the nearest phrase, *to lay hold of folly*, not to the more distant *I searched...to refresh with wine*.

4. A general statement, *I enlarged my works* (NASV), is followed by details. *Houses* recalls the building achievements of Solomon (1 Ki. 7; 9:1; 10:21; 2 Ch. 8:3–6). No mention is made of 'the house of the LORD', for at this point an exclusively 'under the sun' viewpoint is being explored; despite its omission here, 'the house of God' comes into the argument later (5:1–7). *Vineyards* are ascribed to Solomon in the Song of Songs (1:14; 8:11); others may have come to him from David (*cf.* 1 Ch. 27:27). The refrain *for myself*, six times in vv. 4–8, reveals his underlying motivation.

5. Luxurious *gardens* were characteristic of royalty and nobility in the ancient Near East and are attested in Egypt, Mesopotamia and Ugarit. Passing references in the Old Testa-

[1] A. D. Corré takes 'to draw the flesh' to be a reference to epispasm (reversal of circumcision), in conjunction with an emendation which makes *with wine* into 'like the Greeks' ('A Reference to Epispasm in Koheleth', *VT*, 4, 1954, pp. 416–418). *Nāhaḡ* commonly means 'to lead, draw' in the Old Testament, but 'to act, behave' is an attested meaning in Mishnaic writings and seems more suitable here (*cf. DTTML, s.v.*). P. Joüon suggests we read *lᵉsammēᵃḥ* and translate 'to make my heart rejoice' (*Bib*, 11, 1930, p. 419), but more likely *māšak* means 'to stimulate, refresh' as in post-biblical Hebrew, the cognate Aramaic and (according to G. R. Driver, 'Problems and Solutions', *VT*, 4, 1954, pp. 225f.) the cognate Arabic.

ment show that they featured choice plants (Song 5:1; 6:2,11), might contain a summer-house (2 Ki. 9:27) and be walled to ensure privacy (Song 4:12). *Parks* (*pardēsîm*, probably a Persian loan word) is used in Nehemiah 2:8 of a king's parkland large enough to supply timber for building the wall of Jerusalem. Xenophon uses its Greek form (*paradeisos*) of the gardens of Persian kings and nobles.[1]

6. The allusion to *pools* recalls the royal list of achievements of Mesha' of Moab on the Moabite stone (ninth century BC), discovered in 1868: 'It was I who built Qarhoh...its gates...its towers...the king's house...its reservoirs for water.'[2] In Josephus' day the King's Pool in Jerusalem (Ne. 2:14) was thought to be Solomon's.[3] *A forest of growing trees* (NASV) does not refer back to v.5 (implied in RSV by the definite article), but points to an additional luxury; the value of trees for building, making ships and musical instruments, and for shade is often noted in the Old Testament.[4]

7. Two types of *slave*, viewed as an item of wealth, are mentioned: the acquired slave and the child born to parents already in slavery. *Herds and flocks* (RSV), better than *great and small cattle* (AV), recall the daily provisions for Solomon's household (1 Ki. 4:22f.).[5]

8. *Gold* recalls the wealth of Solomon (*cf.* 1 Ki. 10:14–25); *silver* was less highly esteemed (1 Ki. 10:21, NASV), 'as common as stone' (2 Ch. 9:27). The *treasures* were his personal possessions (*cf.* 1 Ch. 29:3)[6] and recalls Solomon's famed wealth.[7] Some see in *provinces* an allusion to Persian rule or to the twelve districts into which Solomon divided his empire (Plumptre, citing 1 Ki. 4:7–19). More likely the reference is to the personal wealth acquired from nearby rulers and subjugated territories (*cf.* 2 Ch. 9). The *singers* were used in banquets (*cf.* 2 Sa. 19:35). *Many concubines* (RSV), a disputed expression, is the singular (*šiddâ*)

---

[1] LS, p. 1308. For further detail, *cf.* K. A. Kitchen, art. 'Garden' and R. K. Harrison, art. 'Vine' in *IBD*, pp. 542 and 1622ff.

[2] *Cf. ANET*, p. 320.

[3] *Jewish Wars* v.4.2; *cf.* J. Wilkinson, 'Ancient Jerusalem. Its Water Supply and Population', *PEQ*, 107, 1974–5, pp. 33–35.

[4] *Cf.* F. N. Hepper, art. 'Trees', *IBD*, pp. 1585–1593.

[5] For the bearing of *any...before me in Jerusalem* upon authorship, see Introduction, p. 24, n.1.

[6] *Cf.* M. Greenberg, 'Hebrew Sᵉgulla: Akkadian Sikiltu', *JAOS*, 71, 1951, pp. 172f. *Sglt* is used similarly in Ugaritic (*cf. PBQ*, p. 267).

[7] For a full survey of the historical evidence for Solomon's great wealth, see A. R. Millard, 'Solomon in all his glory', *Vox Evangelica*, 12, 1981, pp. 5–18.

and plural (*šiddôṯ*) of a word whose meaning has been taken as
(i) cupbearer (LXX, Peshitta), (ii) goblet, drinking-vessel
(Aquila, Vulgate, Targum), (iii) musical instrument (Kimchi,
Luther, AV), (iv) chest (JB, following post-biblical Hebrew) or
(v) mistress, lover, concubine (RSV, NIV, Ibn Ezra and most
modern commentators).[1] The last mentioned is most likely (*cf.*
1 Ki. 11:1–3). As RSV indicates, the singular and plural express
multitude.[2] Kidner cites a letter from Pharaoh Amenophis III
to Milkilu prince of Gezer in which an Egyptian word for
concubine is accompanied by an explanatory Canaanite gloss
akin to *šiddâ*.[3]

9. The picture progresses to the splendour attained by
Solomon. *I became great* refers to his wealth (*cf.* 1 Ki. 10:23).
I...surpassed (RSV) or 'increased' (Heb.) repeats the vocabulary
of the previous section. As he increased in wisdom (1:16, 18), so
he increased in riches (*cf.* 2 Ch. 9:22). Again (*cf.* 2:3) we are
assured that his *wisdom remained with* him. This need not refer
only to the earlier part of Solomon's life (Leupold). Rather it
indicates the breadth of meaning in the word 'wisdom', which
includes the wiles of Pharaoh (Ex. 1:10), the cunning of Jonadab
(2 Sa. 13:3) or the proud self-sufficiency of a king of Assyria (Is.
10:12f.). There is a wisdom which opposes the LORD, yet in vain
(Pr. 21:30); similarly there is nothing godly about the Preacher's
claim here. It simply shows he 'retains his objectivity' (Jones) in
the midst of his pleasures.

10. *Eyes* and *heart* point to the outward and inward aspect of
his pleasures. Nothing was withheld that might be visibly enter-
taining or inwardly satisfying. Most English translations take
the second part of the verse as an explanation: *for my heart found
pleasure* (RSV). It is better, however, to take it as an emphatic
assertion: 'Indeed, my heart found pleasure' (so Aalders,
Hertzberg, Lauha, Lys); NIV achieves this effect. Yet the verse
ends on a darker note. It was the sheer activity that gave
satisfaction; with achievement, the pleasure began to fade.

11. Now he comes to 'the morning after the night before'. *I
considered* (NIV *surveyed*) is literally 'I faced'. The verb means 'to

[1] For other views see Gordis and Lys.
[2] *Cf.* GK 123(c)–(f); Joüon 135(d). Gordis quotes Ibn Ezra's citation of Jdg.
5:30 where 'a maiden and two maidens' is a similar idiom. Possibly the masculine
and feminine (*šarîm, šarôt*) sequence in the same verse is another example of the
same idiom, and should be translated '*many* singers male and female').
[3] The text is in *ANET*, p. 487a.

look someone in the eye' (Jb. 6:28) or (as here) to 'face the facts', 'turn one's full attention'. The Preacher is not content to put a bold face on things; he must tell it the way it is. His *hands*, denoting personal involvement and activity, had kept him pleasurably occupied. The *toil* had been enjoyably strenuous. But in retrospect a verdict passed previously on wisdom (1:17–18) is now applied to pleasure. All the Preacher's key terms combine at this point: *toil, vanity, striving after wind, no profit, under the sun*. The pile-up of terms conveys bitter disillusionment. The morality of his project is not under consideration, for secular man is being shown the failure of his life-style, *on its own premises*.

iv. Life's ultimate certainty (2:12–23). 12.
This verse has perplexed commentators. Its text has often been amended (as in Barton, Gordis, Hertzberg, each in different ways). Others have reversed the clauses so that v.12b is the end of v.11 (so GNB and several nineteenth-century German commentators) or arbitrarily transposed v.12b to the end of v.18 (so NEB) or v.19 (so Lauha). The common English translations insert the word *do* (which strains the Hebrew) and regard v.12b as the answer to the question of v.12a.

The text as it stands may be literally translated, 'And I turned to consider wisdom and madness and folly, for what kind of person[1] is it who will come after the king, in the matter of[2] what has already been done?'[3] 'To turn' means 'to turn one's attention' or 'to take up a new line of thought'. Since the Preacher has thus far shown the complete failure of both wisdom and pleasure-seeking to solve his problem, is there any reason why the king should prefer one to the other? Wisdom is traditionally the special need of the king (1 Ki. 3:5–28; Pr. 8:14–16).[4] But the Preacher has exposed its failure. Does this mean that wisdom fails in all respects? The explanatory phrase deals with the reason why the Preacher, Solomon's ghost writer, should concern him-

---

[1] *What* (*meh*, a variant of *mâh*) may enquire after character, 'What kind of person...?' *Cf.* BDB, pp. 552f.

[2] The Hebrew uses an '*et* of specification'. *Cf.* Aalders who cites 1 Ki. 15:23 (Asa was 'sick *with regard to, in*, his feet') and Jos. 22:17 ('Is it a small thing for us – *with regard to* the sin of Peor – that we have not cleansed ourselves from it?'). *Cf.* also P. P. Saydon, 'Meanings and Uses of the Particle '*t*', *VT*, 14, 1964, pp. 192–210, esp. p. 205; J. Hoftijzer, *OTS*, 14, 1965, pp. 1–99.

[3] Hebrew *'āśûhû* ('they do') may be taken impersonally '...has been done'.

[4] *Cf.* D. A. Hubbard, art. 'Wisdom', *IBD*, p. 1650; N. W. Porteous, 'Royal Wisdom', *WIANE*, pp. 247 ff.

self with the question whether wisdom is of any value at all. We may paraphrase: 'How will future kings handle the same problem I have faced? What kind of person will my successor be in his attitude to the same problems I have had to deal with?' This coheres with the Preacher's concern for the future, mentioned elsewhere (1:9–11; 2:18f., 21; 3:22; 7:14).

13. The question receives a twofold answer. First, *wisdom* is of value. At this point the traditional doctrine is conceded. The Preacher's critique is not of wisdom in every respect, but as the ultimate source of reliance. 'Ecclesiastes is the frontier-guard who forbids Wisdom to cross the frontier towards the comprehensive art of life... The fear of God never allows man in his "art of directing" to hold the helm in his own hands.'[1] Thus reduced to size, wisdom is like *light* to a man walking. This is common imagery.[2] To possess wisdom will give success (10:10), preserve life and protect (7:12). It gives strength (7:19) and joy (8:1), and is better than mere brute strength (9:16). Man is guided by it (2:3), toils by it (2:21), tests and weighs experiences by it (7:23). Even the practical politics of delivering cities involves wisdom (9:15). Limited it may be, but it is still indispensable.

14. The Preacher now considers wisdom from the angle of its recipient. As God's gift it is light; as man's possession it is sight. *The fool* (*kᵉsîl*) whom we meet here for the first time is 'notorious for his babbling, his drunkenness, his tendency to evil'[3], one for whom wickedness is 'fun' (Pr. 10:23) and who has more interest in his own pursuits than in wisdom (Pr. 18:2). He too is characterized from two angles. He has no 'light' from God, no 'eyes' in himself. He prefigures the New Testament sinner who *loves* darkness (Jn. 3:19) and *is* darkness (Eph. 5:8).

The second part of the answer follows. As a cure for the ultimate problem of life, wisdom is useless; both the wise man and the fool succumb to death. AV *event* is a good translation. The underlying word (*miqreh*) is sometimes translated *fate* (RSV and NIV), giving the impression of a 'strange fatalistic concept of God' (Hertzberg). The Hebrew word is entirely neutral and has no sinister nuance. It occurs seven times in Ecclesiastes (2:14, 15; 3:19, three times; 9:2, 3) and three times elsewhere (Ru. 2:3;

---

[1] W. Zimmerli, *SJT*, 17, 1964, p. 158.
[2] *Cf.* O. A. Piper, art. 'Light', *IDB*, vol. 3, p. 131.
[3] *Cf.* T. Donald, 'The Semantic Field of "Folly" in Proverbs, Job, Psalms, and Ecclesiastes', *VT*, 13, 1963, pp. 285–292. A fuller characterization of 'the fool' is found under 10:3–4.

1 Sa. 6:9; 20:26). The associated verb occurs three times in
Ecclesiastes (2:14, 15; 9:11) and nineteen elsewhere. It may be
used of calamities which 'happen' to people (Gn. 42:29; 44:29; 1
Sa. 28:10; Est. 4:7; 6:13) or of happy events, as when God's word
'happens', *i.e.* 'comes true' (Nu. 11:23). It is used of the
Amalekites aggressively 'meeting' the Israelites on their journey
to Canaan (Dt. 25:18) and of the LORD graciously 'meeting'
Israel in blessing (Ex. 3:18). Abraham's servant is 'made to
meet' with success (Gn. 24:12; *cf.* Gn. 27:20). Moses must
'cause to come into being' cities of refuge (Nu. 35:11). In Daniel
10:14 it refers to future events which 'shall happen' in the
purpose of God (*cf.* Is. 41:22). In 2 Samuel 1:6 a young man
claims he 'happened' to be on Mount Gilboa as Saul was dying.
None of these carries any arbitrary, fatalistic overtone. A
Philistine can speak of something happening 'by accident' (1
Sa. 6:9); the surrounding narrative puts a different light on the
matter. On the lips of an Israelite 'chance' means what is
unexpected, not what is random. Hebrew *miqreh* means 'something that happens'. In Ruth 2, the Moabitess 'happens' to
come to Boaz's field, an event unplanned and unexpected, as
emphasized in the Hebrew of v.3 (*wayyiqer miqrehā*); yet Naomi
blesses God for what happened (v.20), and the over-all thrust of
the book of Ruth is that the event was far from the arbitrary
whim of chance.

In Ecclesiastes *miqreh* (or *qārāh*) refers almost always to the
'event' of death that will 'happen' to all men. On one occasion
(9:11) the verb refers to what is totally unexpected from man's
viewpoint. It would be a mistake to read into it a picture of God
in which he is indifferent or distant. In the next verse (2:15) *what
befalls* (RSV) is correct.

15. The inevitability of death makes the quest for wisdom
seem pointless, for death is the great leveller. The Preacher
notes this after his pursuit for wisdom, not before. The grass
looked greener from the other side of the fence. *Then* refers to
logical consequence: 'in that case'.[1]

16. A point previously made with regard to history in general
(1:16) is now repeated with regard to people: memories are too
short to make human endeavours worth while (*cf.* 9:5). A contrasting point is made in Proverbs 10:7 and Psalm 112:6, from the
standpoint of faith. RSV *just like* is 'in common with' (*cf.* Gn. 18:23).

[1] *Cf.* BDB, p. 23.

17. From here to v.23 the Preacher considers the results of all that has been seen from 1:2 onwards. It is *life* as a whole that interests him (*cf.* 2:3; 6:12; 8:15). But every aspect of it so far has proved hateful. If death brings wisdom to a halt, it also throws back its dark shadow upon life itself. *Grievous* means 'calamitous' (as in 1:13; Gn. 47:9; Pr. 15:10). *To me* may be correct (as Delitzsch and Barton emphasize), but the Hebrew expression may mean 'upon me' and sometimes expresses that which is burdensome (*cf.* Is. 1:14).[1]

Later, life will be portrayed in different terms. From a God-centred viewpoint it is a time to enjoy good (3:12; 5:20), because it is given by God (5:18); its pleasures are part of one's portion from God (9:9). But that position cannot be reached from 'under the sun'.

18. Hatred of life is followed by hatred of *toil* (contrast 9:9 with its portion to be enjoyed 'all the days of your life...and in your labour'). *Toil* varies in meaning within Ecclesiastes; sometimes it refers to one's whole struggle with the problem of life (1:13), sometimes (as here) to one's daily responsibilities. Work must be left behind, so what is the point of it? The Preacher is neither denying nor affirming an afterlife at this point; he is concerned with wisdom as an aid in a world dominated by futility. *Leave* is more precisely 'bequeath' (JB).[2]

19. A man may ruin the work of his predecessor. There is no guarantee that another will carry on the good work. It is doubtful that there is any direct reference to Rehoboam (1 Ki. 11:41 – 12:24), but he aptly illustrates the point.

20. All hope of a worth-while life has been swallowed up. Wisdom (1:12–18) and pleasure (2:1–11) have failed. Wisdom has its terminus (2:12–15). Human endeavour cannot be remembered (2:16), retained (2:18) or passed on (2:19). The only conclusion is that it is all useless. An abyss of despair results. He 'allowed [his] heart to despair' (as the Hebrew verb may be translated).[3] This is one of the most moving points of the Old Testament, the antithesis of the New Testament's 'not in vain in the Lord' (1 Cor. 15:58).

21. Here all endeavour is said to be even worse than useless!

---

[1] *Cf.* BDB, p. 755.
[2] Hiphil of *nûaḥ* (*cf.* BDB, pp. 628 f.).
[3] The permissive force of the piel (*cf.* GK 52g) is suitable here. The verb *yā'aš* is used in later writings for abandoning all hope (*cf. DTTML, s.v.*). GNB fails to convey the note of despair.

It actually seems an injustice that another should benefit from his predecessor's labours. Though accompanied by *wisdom* (practical know-how), *knowledge* (information) and *skill* (expertise, better than AV *equity*), there is nothing that can sidestep death or guarantee permanence. *Skill* (*kišrôn*), the success that derives from practical know-how (*cf.* 4:4) is sometimes translated 'advantage', 'gain', 'success'.

22. The Preacher begins to wind up the whole argument from 1:2 onwards. Actual *toil* and emotional-intellectual struggles (*striving of his heart*, AV) prove equally useless.

23. Phrases like *all his days*, which recur intermittently throughout the book (*cf.* 2:3; 5:17–18; 6:3, 12; 8:15; 9:9; 11:9; 12:1), show that the Preacher is concerned not with detailed problems but with our view of life as a whole. The opening words of the Hebrew may be 'All his days are sorrows and his work a vexation' (*cf.* RSV) or 'All his days, his work is sorrows and vexation' (*cf.* NIV). The difference is negligible. The two terms 'sorrow' and 'vexation' reiterate the conclusion of 1:18. Both may refer to mental and physical anguish. The former is in view here, but sleepless nights are a physical side-effect, for the restlessness of the 'under the sun' world-view reveals itself *even in the night*. A different perspective appears in 5:12; in the New Testament we find a Messiah who could sleep in a storm (Mk. 4:38) and enable his disciples to do likewise (Acts 12:6).

C. THE ALTERNATIVE TO PESSIMISM: FAITH IN GOD (2:24 – 3:22)

There are good reasons for seeing a major turning-point at 2:24. Three aspects of the contrast may be highlighted.

(i) God is scarcely mentioned in 1:1 – 2:23. The only allusion to God is in 1:13, not as the answer to mankind's problem but as its cause ('the travail *God* gave to the sons of men'). The world is 'subjected to vanity, not of its own will' but of God's will (*cf.* Rom. 8:20). That, however, is no solution; it only deepens the problem. 2:24, however, introduces 'the other side to the unhappy business' (Kidner) and a new note is added. The argument in 1:1 – 2:23 is dominated by qualifying phrases confining our vision to the earthly realm (1:3, 13f.; 2:3, 11, 17–20, 22). In the following section, however, God is often in view. He is the source of wisdom, knowledge and joy. He is a just governor of sinner and righteous alike. He controls the cosmos not simply to guarantee its structures and its being 'subjected unto vanity' (1:13; *cf.* 3:10), but also as the originator of beauty (3:11).

(ii) There is a difference in the way wisdom is viewed. In 1:16 it is man's acquisition; in 2:26 it is God's gift. Though these are complementary statements and are not necessarily to be put in opposition (*cf.* Pr. 2:1–6), it is significant that no reference to God's gift has been made hitherto. In 2:21 'wisdom and knowledge' are found in company with 'skill', yet judged a failure; in 2:26 they are found in company with 'joy' and considered a blessing.

(iii) In the earlier sections the argument has been entirely nihilistic. The Preacher's review of creation, history, life and death has ended in a picture of physical and mental anguish. There is no allusion to beauty, justice or joy. But in 2:24 – 3:22 we have reference to enjoyment (2:25), beauty (3:11), God's gifts (3:13), security (3:14), a divine purpose in the midst of injustice (3:18) and joy despite injustice (3:22). Mankind is to enjoy the created realm. He receives such enjoyment from the hand of God. Sinner and righteous are appropriately handled by God who disposes the order of every matter under heaven. The authority which guarantees the emptiness of secularism (*cf.* 1:13) also guarantees the fruitfulness of the life of faith.

We conclude on exegetical grounds that 2:24 marks a turning-point in the argument. Coherent exposition is possible if this antithesis is accepted. Having exposed the bankruptcy of our pretended autonomy, the Preacher now points to the God who occupies the heavenly realm, and to the life of faith in him.

The section begins and ends with the enjoyment of the earthly realm (2:24; 3:22; *cf.* 3:13). The themes of divine authority (2:26; 3:1–8, 17), human need (2:26; 3:10a, 13, 18–20) and joys of life (2:24; 3:12–13, 22) form connecting links. 3:16–22, however, has links in two directions. To view the enigmas of life in the light of a divine judgment forms a fitting end to 2:24 – 3:15, yet the theme of unjust suffering also leads into 4:1–3 and so into the remainder of the book.

i. The life of faith (2:24–26). A new view of life appears. The 'under the sun' limitation is left aside; in contrast the hand of God is seen in human affairs.

24. Firstly, for the Preacher with his new viewpoint, life is to

73

be enjoyed: 'There is nothing better for a man than that he eat and drink and cause himself to enjoy[1] his work.' Four proverbs in Ecclesiastes take the form *There is nothing better than* ... (2:24; 3:12, 22; 8:15). Each is an 'animated affirmation'[2] that mankind has no higher good than to synchronize with God's beneficent purposes for him. To *eat and drink* signifies contentment.[3]

The earthly realm is essentially good and meant for our enjoyment (*cf*. Gn. 2:9). Similarly, human endeavour is to be enjoyed. So the Preacher reverts to the orthodox Israelite view of the created realm: God 'brings forth food from the earth, and wine to gladden the heart of man, oil to make his face shine, and bread to strengthen man's heart' (Ps. 104:14f.). W. Eichrodt speaks of 'this exaltation in the Old Testament of earthly possessions, many children, long life, friendship and love, as well as wisdom, beauty, honour and political freedom ... When human life is thus surrounded and upheld by God's blessed will, man's basic mood in relation to his task and his destiny is one of joy. As God's pleasure in his works is recounted in Psalms (Ps. 104:31; *cf*. Gn. 1, with its emphasis on "And God saw that it was good") which but repeat the praise and jubilation of the morning stars and all the sons of God on the morning of creation (Jb. 38:7), which in fact see the world as a joyous game of God's wisdom, so joy is seen as man's portion from God (Ec. 2:26; 8:15; 9:7; 11:9f).'[4]

The Preacher is not advising worldliness. His attitude is to be distinguished from the covetousness of the rich fool (Lk. 12:16–21) or the exclusively mundane horizon of the unbeliever (1 Cor. 15:32); he recommends not licentiousness or scepticism, but contentment. Its New Testament parallel is 1 Timothy 4:4; 6:6–8.

25. Secondly, such a life is the gift of God. 'Under the sun' life leads to despair; we now have the opposite and balancing truth: *For who eats and who has enjoyment without him?* 'To eat' is used as an indicator of a prosperous life.[5] Two exegetical decisions are involved in our translation. The latter verb (*ḥûš*)

---

[1] *Cf*. p.64 for a note on the meaning of 'see' in Ecclesiastes.
[2] The term is G. S. Ogden's. *Cf*. his 'Qoheleth's Use of the "Nothing is Better"-Form', *JBL*, 98, 1979, pp. 339–350.
[3] See further 5:18 and comments there.
[4] W. Eichrodt, *Man in the Old Testament* (1951), p. 337.
[5] See further, p.103.

may mean (i) enjoy,[1] (ii) worry, be anxious,[2] (iii) refrain,[3] (iv) eat, gorge oneself;[4] of these the first best fits the context, and on this view *ḥûš* is a variant of *ḥāšaš*.[5] Our translation also assumes that the text should read *mimmennû* (*apart from him*, RSV; *cf.* NIV, *etc.*) instead of MT *mimmennî* ('without me'; *cf.* RV *more than I*). This is almost universally accepted by modern commentators; LXX assumes it. There is ample evidence that Hebrew *-û* was often confused with *-î*; in the Qumran manuscripts it is sometimes quite impossible to tell which is intended.[6]

26. Thirdly, as a general rule (for the verbs here may denote customary action), *God bestows gifts of wisdom, knowledge and joy on the man who pleases him.* The Preacher shows how the enjoyment of vv.24f. comes about: by living so as to please God and by receiving his gifts (*cf.* Heb. 11:6). Three are itemized. *Wisdom*, as given by God, he evaluates highly. It enables a man to walk without stumbling (2:14), it gives success (10:10), preserves life (7:12) and protects (7:12), enables successful toil (2:21) and discriminating judgments (7:23), is required for all great human endeavour (9:15) and gives strength (7:19; 9:16) and joy (8:1). *Knowledge* is not simply the acquisition of facts; it includes experience of life. *Joy* is the soundly-based, reasonable exultation in God and life's blessings (*cf.* 2:1–2, and comments on *śimḥâ*).

The *sinner*, however, is in a totally different position. For him the *task* ('*inyan*, 'business', 'occupation') of 1:13 is unrelieved. Thrown into existence willy-nilly, he has no way of coping with his perplexities or with his aching desire for a sense of direction. He is left with his projects and his quest for meaning – plus

---

[1] This is the most widely accepted explanation and is adopted by G. Bickell, *Der Prediger Über Den Wert Daseins* (1884); G. Wildeboer, *Der Prediger* (1898); M. Thilo, *Der Prediger* (1923); H. Odeberg, *Qohaelaeth* (1923); W. Zimmerli, *Das Buch Des Predigers Salomo* (1962), as well as McNeile, Hertzberg, Aalders, Lys and others. Dahood cites evidence from Akkadian and Ugaritic (*cf.* QRD, pp. 307f.).

2 This is the view of the study by F. Ellermeier, 'Das Verbum *Ḥûš* in Koh. 2:25', *ZATW*, 75, 1963, pp. 197–217; and his *Qohelet*, Teil 1, Abschnitt 2 (1970); G. R. Driver, 'Studies in the Vocabulary of the Old Testament, III', *JTS*, 32, 1931, pp. 253f.

[3] So Gordis.

[4] So J. Reider, 'Etymological Studies in Biblical Hebrew', *VT*, 2, 1952, pp. 129f.

[5] Thus *ḥûš* is related to *ḥāšaš*, just as *rûm* has the same meaning as *rāmam*.

[6] Dahood believes that a 3rd person singular suffix *-î* exists in Hebrew, and that without emendation the meaning is 'without Him' (PBQ, p. 269; *Psalms*, vol. 3 (1970), p. 375).

nothing! Although later all men are said to commit sin (7:20), at this point there is a clear contrast between *the man who pleases him* and *the sinner*. *Sinner*, therefore, has a limited reference (*cf.* Gal. 2:15): he is one who does not take his life from the hand of God. No specific breaking of God's law is mentioned; the Preacher is concerned with world-view, not morality.

The sinner's position is no mishap or coincidence but a judgment; *he* (*i.e.* God) *gives* it. So the sinner occupies himself (*'inyan*, from *'ānāh*, 'to be busy', 'to occupy oneself'), he *gathers* (*'āsap̄*, elsewhere used of gathering food, Gn. 6:21; sheep, Gn. 29:7; and belongings, Je. 10:17; as well as money, 2 Ch. 24:11), and he *collects* (*kānas*, elsewhere used of collecting contributions, first-fruits and tithes, Ne. 12:4, as well as silver and gold, Ec. 2:8). The verbs here have no object (NIV *wealth* is not explicit in the Hebrew), giving the impression of all-embracing acquisitiveness. The sinner gathers not simply wealth, but possessions, projects, ideas, friends, fame, and more besides. But he himself does not get 'gain' (*cf.* 1:3) as a result. Rather everything, even the produce of the *sinner*, is to the benefit of *the one who pleases God*. How this occurs is never spelt out, and it is perhaps significant that the Preacher's frequent 'I have seen' is not found here. It may be this unanswered question that leads into ch. 3, with its assertion that the 'times and seasons' of life are in God's hands. Elsewhere we find the principle, 'The sinner's wealth is laid up for the righteous' (Pr. 13:22; *cf.* 28:8). Occasional incidents (Mordecai receiving Haman's signet ring, the Canaanites' 'great and goodly cities' falling into Israel's hands) give a glimpse of what the Preacher had in mind. The New Testament takes the principle further (Mt. 5:5; Lk. 19:24; 1 Cor. 3:21; 2 Cor. 6:10). Here it remains a position of faith, for the Preacher himself points to life's injustices (3:16–22, *etc.*). It is unlikely that the last phrase means that the satisfaction and joy of vv.24–26a are *striving after wind*. Rather it is a further comment on the plight of the *sinner*. *This too* may be translated 'This indeed' (for the Hebrew *gam* may be used for emphasis as well as for addition).[1]

Here then is the antithesis of secular pessimism. The Preacher has held before his readers two ways of life: the vicious circle of a pointless world, temporary pleasures, fruitless work, futile wisdom, inevitable death, versus an enjoyable life taken daily from the hand of God, in the 'assurance of faith' that he deals

---

[1] *Cf.* BDB, p. 169.

appropriately with righteous and unrighteous.

ii. The providence of God (3:1–15). This section elucidates the world-view underlying the life portrayed in 2:24–26. Just as 1:2 – 2:23 moved from the pessimistic world-view (1:2–11) to the pessimistic daily life (1:12 – 2:23), so in a chiastic movement the thought of 2:24–26 proceeds from the believer's life to his world-view (3:1–22). Verses 1–8 lay down the basic postulate; 9–15 work out its practical implications.

This reading takes 3:1–15 as orthodox, not, as has often been maintained, as part of the Preacher's despair. Jones is one of many who maintain that 'although the passage is one of great beauty and poetry, the burden is that of protest...Its essence is that Koheleth feels imprisoned by this sequence of times, and he rebels because this is what he must go through, though without knowing why'. H. L. Ginsberg similarly sees the Preacher as a fatalist whose rigid predestinarianism is an obstruction to the quest for a satisfying life; it is an example of men's striving 'to anticipate his time-table, but without their ever guessing everything correctly...Koheleth regards God as the absolute and arbitrary master of destiny'.[1] James Barr says that it is 'clear that the purpose of the whole is to emphasize the frustrating effect of time on human life and labour, whether because God has appointed the events beforehand or for some other reason'.[2]

This is part of the truth, as indicated by certain conclusions in vv.9–15. Verses 9, 10 and 11b stress human inadequacy under God's disposal of the epochs of life. Events and characteristic seasons of time are imposed upon men: no-one chooses a time to weep. Equally, the events of life that come our way undermine our confidence that our endeavours will have any permanence. 'Whatever may be our skill and initiative, our real masters seem to be these inexorable seasons: not only those of the calendar, but that tide of events which moves us now to one kind of action which seems fitting, now to another which puts it all into reverse.'[3] We are not sure they will have any total meaning, and we cannot stand outside the events of life and view them 'from the beginning to the end'. All this puts mankind in his place, far from being master of his fate and captain of his soul.

However, there is more than one conclusion in these verses.

---

[1] *WIANE*, pp. 140, 147.
[2] James Barr, *Biblical Words for Time* (1962), p. 99.
[3] Kidner, p. 38.

Verses 11a, 12–15 stress that the disposal of events which humiliates men may also be the ground of their joy and security. This section may, therefore, have quite another force, contributing to the Preacher's *solution* of the problem of life's vanity. C. S. Knopf is surely right: 'too often the whole cast of the book has been determined by certain pessimistic elements, ignoring just as patent constructive elements...Chapter three has often been interpreted as a lament of the ceaseless round of life. Instead it is part of the basic optimism of Koheleth.'[1]

1. The Old Testament commonly sees purposefulness in life coming from God's providential oversight of its occasions and seasons. Each aspect of life has its 'time': rain (Lv. 26:4), the downfall of God's enemies (Dt. 32:35), conception (2 Ki. 4:16f.). Hence the great need of 'insight into times' (1 Ch. 12:32; *cf.* Ec. 8:5). Wisdom involves knowing 'the times' (Est. 1:13); godliness says 'My times are in your hands' (Ps. 31:15). The Preacher holds a similar viewpoint: the 'times' of life cannot be fully known (9:11f.) but 'in all time' (9:8) one should be content.

'Every event', says von Rad, 'has its definite place in the time-order; the event is inconceivable without its time, and vice-versa.'[2] 'God is intimately connected with time,' says H. W. Robinson; '...His relation to men itself requires the time-order for the fulfillment of His purposes.'[3] This approach to time which permeates the Old Testament[4] is taken up by the Preacher and made the basis of his optimism. The fourteen couplets of 3:2–8 cover the whole range of human activity. Over it all the Preacher sees God in complete control. It is a warrant at the same time for both humility and confidence.

Time simply means an 'occasion' or a 'season' of time; *purpose* pinpoints what one wants to do. Elsewhere it is used of one's *pleasure* (5:4; 12:1 and the Hebrew of 12:10). The pairing of the varying aspects of human life indicates the universality of God's control. For the expression of totality in pairs is a common Old Testament idiom.[5] Thus 'man and woman' (Ex. 36:6) or 'great

[1] C. S. Knopf, 'The Optimism of Koheleth', *JBL*, 49, 1930, p. 195.
[2] G. von Rad, *Theology of the Old Testament*, vol. 2 (1965), p. 100.
[3] H. W. Robinson, *Revelation and Inspiration in the Old Testament* (1946), p. 112.
[4] *Cf.* Gn. 18:10, 14; 31:10; 38:27; 2 Ch. 18:34; 28:22; Ezr. 10:13–14; Ne. 9:27; 10:34; Jb. 5:26; 24:1; 38:23, 32; 39:1–2; Pss. 1:3; 9:9; 10:1; 104:27; 145:15; Pr. 15:23; Song 2:12; Is. 49:8; Je. 5:24; 8:7, 15; 14:19; 15:11; 30:7; 51:6, 18, 33; Ezk. 21:25; 30:3; Mi. 5:3; Hg. 1:2.
[5] See further C. H. Gordon, *The World of the Old Testament* (1960), p. 35; A. M. Honeyman, 'Merismus in Biblical Hebrew', *JBL*, 71, 1952, pp. 11–18.

and small' (Je. 6:13) is used to say emphatically 'everybody'; 'sea and land' (Jon. 1:9) is an emphatic way of saying 'everywhere'.

2–3. The most momentous events of human life are mentioned first: childbearing and death. The Hebrew here is active (*to give birth*, NASV); it is doubtful whether it can be taken passively (*to be born*, AV, RSV), although Jeremiah 25:34 is sometimes cited as an example of an active infinitive with passive force ('your being slaughtered', Heb.)

The next three pairs deal with various creative and destructive human activities. Each of the six verbs may be figuratively used for establishing or undermining. 'Planting the heavens' (Is. 51:16) indicates permanence and stability.[1] *Uproot* or 'harvest'[2] is used figuratively elsewhere of destroying a nation (Zp. 2:4; *cf.* the Aramaic of Dn. 7:8). *Kill* probably falls in line with this pattern (*cf.* its figurative use in Jb. 5:2; Pr. 1:32; 7:26). Certainly *heal* does not always refer to medical needs (*cf.* Is. 6:10 following up the imagery of 1:5–6; Is. 19:22; 57:19; Je. 33:6 and often elsewhere). *Tear down* is applied to the LORD when Jehoshaphat's schemes were ruined (2 Ch. 20:37; *cf.* Ps. 60:1). *Build* is applied to the throne of David, the city of Zion, and to the land of Judah, as well as to literal construction work (*cf.* Pss. 89:4; 102:16). The widespread figurative uses of these verbs strongly suggest they were chosen here to express not only specific activities but all the manifold pursuits of men, creative and destructive, good and evil, benevolent and malevolent. Mankind is not self-sufficient in these activities; he is within the control of God.

4. The next two pairs incorporate human emotions, first private (*weep...laugh*), then public (*lament...dance*).

5. The following two pairs deal with friendship and enmity. Four major views have been held of *to throw stones...to gather stones*: (i) The Aramaic Targum of Ecclesiastes saw a reference to scattering stones on an old building and preparing to build a new one; this was held also by Ibn Ezra.[3] (ii) Others see a reference to rendering fields unproductive by covering its surface with stones (*cf.* 2 Ki. 3:19, 25; Is. 5:2). (iii) Plumptre saw here an 'old Jewish practice...of flinging stones or earth into the grave at the burial' in the first phrase, and preparation to build a

[1] This assumes the correction of MT at this point. The text however is not entirely certain (*cf.* RSV).
[2] There is Phoenician evidence that 'harvest' is a possible meaning (*cf.* PBQ, p. 270).
[3] *Cf.* A. Sperber, *The Bible in Aramaic*, vol, IV A (1968), p. 153.

house, in the second. (iv) More recent scholars have seen a sexual reference following the Midrashic interpretation (*cf.* GNB). The first three possibilities have often been rejected on the ground that they 'leave the second half of the verse without any logical connection' (Jones). But the second half need not have an exclusively 'passionate meaning' (Jones); possibly it alludes merely to showing friendship or enmity. If so, it is likely that the first pair puts the same point in national or military terms. 'Gathering stones together' will refer to preparing the way for a military conqueror (*cf.* Is. 62:10); casting stones will refer to military aggression by ruining an enemy's fields.

6. The next two pairs reflect on possessions and our resolutions concerning them: *to search* (better than AV *get*)...*to give up* (as lost);[1]...*to keep*...*to throw away* (NIV).

7–8. Some scholars consider that the next pair (*tearing... sewing together*) refers to mourning and the termination of mourning. There is, however, no specific evidence that 'sewing together' was an expression for the end of mourning. It may be better to take it as a general expression for the varying activities of man, destructive and creative (as in vv.2b, 3a, 3b, 6). The remaining couplets incorporate human speech (*to be silent...to speak*), affections (*love...hate*) and national endeavours (*war... peace*) under the pervasive control of divinely arranged times.

9. The first eight verses have asserted a providential control of life, but with little interpretation or comment. There has been no mention of the God who initiates and controls this scheme of 'times', nor has its relevance to daily life been elucidated. Verses 9–15 rectify that twin omission. The elucidation is both pessimistic and optimistic. It holds out confirmation of the hope of 2:24–26, and yet also confirms the dark alternative, the pessimism of 1:2 – 2:23. The thrust of the passage is that man is offered a life that is joyful but not self-sufficient. The initial relevance of the sovereignty of God over earthly 'times' is to confirm the profitlessness of human life. In other words no-one is put into such a superior position that for him the 'vanity' of life does not exist; the problem of 1:3 is not entirely abolished.

10. The Preacher's survey is no longer limited to 'under the sun'; the working of God is brought into consideration. The passing mention of God's activity in 1:13 receives fuller explanation.[2]

---

[1] The permissive use of piel fits here, as NIV perceives.

[2] GNB translates *fate* in 1:13, although the Hebrew word (*'inyan*, 'task') is not

11. His view of the earthly realm is that God's disposal of events in their 'times' is *beautiful* (*yāpeh*). The adjective is generally applied to beauty of appearance (Gn. 12:11). Far from being grounds for despair, the 'times' of earthly events are a source of delight.

God has set *eternity* in men's hearts. This expression has been taken to mean (i) eternity (RSV, LXX), (ii) the world (Mishnah, AV), (iii) ignorance (revocalizing *'elem*), (iv) darkness (on the basis of an Ugaritic root).[1] 'Eternity', by far the commonest meaning, fits the context well, for the whole passage has been concerned with God's scheme of 'times'. Yet his actions endure *for ever* (14). The 'eternity' in man's heart must be connected with the 'eternity' of v.14. 'Eternity' was important in Israel's heritage. An eternal life had been lost (Gn. 3:22), an 'eternal covenant' inaugurated (Gn. 9:16) by an eternal God (Ps. 90:2). An eternal priesthood (Ex. 40:15) and an eternal kingdom (2 Sa. 7:13) were bestowed by a God eternally merciful (Ps. 111:5), giving his people eternal joy (Is. 35:10). The eternity of God's dealings with mankind corresponds to something inside us: we have a capacity for eternal things, are concerned about the future, want to understand 'from the beginning to the end', and have a sense of something which transcends our immediate situation. Scripture speaks of our creation in the 'image' or 'glory' of God (Gn. 1:26f.), a glory which is largely forfeited (Rom. 3:23) yet not obliterated (1 Cor. 11:7; Jas. 3:9). Our consciousness of God is part of our nature, and the suppression of it is part of our sin (Rom. 1:18–21).

This inward 'eternity' has a negative result: *man does not find out the work God has done from the beginning to the end* (cf. NIV). The Preacher's vast researches have found nothing in the finite earthly realm which can satisfy the human heart intellectually or practically. Though he has resolved to understand 'all' that is under the sun (1:13), there is that within him which makes him realize he can never comprehend God's plan in its entirety (*from beginning to end*, NIV). This is the nearest he comes to Augustine's maxim: 'You have made us for yourself, and our hearts are restless until they can find peace in you.'[2]

---

the same as GNB *fate* in 2:14. In neither case is it a good translation. See pp. 62, 69-70.

[1] *Cf.* Dahood, CPIQ, p. 206; J. Gray, *The Legacy of Canaan*, *VTS*, 5, 1965, p. 274; and Jones.

[2] *Confessions* i.1.

12. Verses 12–15 divide into two units beginning *I know*. The first holds out again hope of an enjoyable life from the hand of God (12f.); the second shows the security of such a life is its divine guarantor (14f.). The first sees such a life as man's privilege; the second as God's purpose. Thus 2:24 – 3:15 runs full circle.

The Preacher's earlier pursuit of pleasure, to 'enjoy what is good' (2:1) arrived at only a dismal conclusion. Now he maintains that we can enjoy good (*cf*. 2:24, 26) and even bring it about. The active pursuit of genuine and satisfying enjoyment is opened up to him. 'To do good' does not have its modern philanthropic sense. From the context it clearly includes the enjoyment of life (*cf*. RSV), and means actively to pursue and practise a good and happy life.[1]

13. In the material realm the Preacher specifies food and drink, tokens of a contented and happy life (*cf*. comments on 2:24). Daily toil, before pleasurable and vexatious at the same time (2:10f.), is now described only in terms of enjoyment. The decisive new factor is the sovereignty of God. Secularism gives way to theism, pessimism to optimism, human autonomy to human faith.

14. The thought turns to the security of the believer's life. Earth is beset with futility, transitoriness, unreliability (1:2f.); security must be found elsewhere, in God's grace and sovereignty over it. Three aspects of God's action are highlighted. First, it is permanent; the Preacher allows no possibility of failure in him. Second, it is effective and complete; none of his works has to be abandoned. Third, his actions are totally secure; no part or aspect can be endangered by any alien force. All this leads on the part of man to *fear*, not a craven terror in the face of the monstrous or the unknown, but rather the opposite, reverence and awesome regard for God (*cf*. 5:7; 12:13).

15. The opening phrase appeared in 1:9–11, indicating the permanent hopelessness of secular man's situation. Now similar expressions affirm the security of his hope. It is *God* who keeps the cycles of nature and history going: the believer's hope is as immutable as the pessimist's despair.

An addition is found here which is not found in 1:9–11: *God*

---

[1] *Cf*. BDB, p. 795. The phrase also has links with covenant terminology (*cf*. D. J. Wiseman, 'Law and Order in the Old Testament', *Vox Evangelica*, 8, 1973, pp. 12, 20) but in Ecclesiastes this would probably be no more than a vague association.

seeks what is pursued or it might be translated '…what hurries along'. The verb (*rdp*) normally means 'pursue' or 'persecute'. It is difficult, however, to make sense of the passage with either. Many solutions have been offered: (i) It has been taken to refer to past events (AV *what is passed*; RSV *driven away*; NASV and Berkeley *passed by*) or to God's bringing past events back into being again (NEB *God summons each event back*; cf. Moffatt and GNB). (ii) NIV *will call the past to account* makes it refer to judgment, a fitting preliminary to 3:16–22. (iii) NAB *restores what would otherwise be displaced* stretches the Hebrew somewhat. (iv) JB *cares for the persecuted* is a legitimate translation of the Hebrew and follows LXX and Ben Sira (5:3), but scarcely fits the context. (v) Nor is it adequate to emend the text (with Galling)[1] or remove it to the end of v.17 (with Graetz).[2]

A different solution seems preferable. The passive/reflexive of the verb is used here but scarcely anywhere else in the Old Testament (only in La. 5:5 where it means 'persecuted'). In later Hebrew the passive participle sometimes lost its force and meant 'quick, rapid'. It is used, for example, of a stream which 'runs rapidly'.[3] If, then, the verb has lost its passive meaning, it could mean 'hurry along'. This fits well with 1:5–8 where the same vocabulary is used for the world hurrying around its circuits (cf. 1:9).[4] *Seeks* indicates God's watchful concern.

Earlier, earthly events were portrayed as rushing along a determined course (1:5–7). Now comes an explanation: the source of earthly movement is God himself. In 1:13 the 'unhappy business' of man's life was inevitable, said the Preacher, since a divine appointment lay behind it. In 3:1–8 the structure of 'times' was seen as a God-ordained pattern in human life. Likewise in 3:15 the hubbub of human activity is guaranteed and secure because God watches over it all every moment with providential concern.

iii. The judgment of God (3:16–22).
This unit makes an observation (v.16), passes two comments (17, 18–21) and reaches a conclusion (22) (*I saw…I said…I said…So I saw*). The pattern

[1] Cf. *Handbuch zum Alten Testament*, 18, 1969, p. 93.
[2] A fuller survey of interpretation is found in R. B. Salters, 'A Note on the Exegesis of Ecclesiastes 3 15b', *ZATW*, 88, 1976, pp. 419f.
[3] Cf. *DTTML, s.v.*
[4] On niphal forms with 'middle voice' meanings, cf. M. H. Segal, *A Grammar of Mishnaic Hebrew* (1958), p. 59.

of observation (*I saw*) followed by comments (*I said*) is found several times in Ecclesiastes (2:13–25; 7:25–27; 8:14f.).

16. Taking a fresh line of thought (*And furthermore...*) the Preacher bluntly presents an observable (*I saw*) problem of life. At places where judicial procedure is in progress and where uprightness of character (*righteousness*) might be expected, wickedness is often found instead. He has specific instances in mind, for he has seen them; but the description is unspecific because it is the general moral perversion of the world that is brought to view. Hengstenberg recalls Jehoshaphat's warnings (2 Ch. 19:6f.).

17. The Preacher first reflects (*I said in my heart*) on earthly injustice in the light of a future (*will*), divine (*God will*), event (*there is a time*), a coming judgment. The term suggests not merely judicial assessment but the execution of sentence also, for in the Old Testament 'to judge' includes this dynamic element.[1] This sustains the Preacher in his perplexity, as it did Abraham (Gn. 18:25) and the psalmist (Ps. 73:17). This coming event is all-embracing, for it includes *the righteous and the wicked*; it assesses both *purpose* (AV, probably better in this context than RSV *matter*) and deed (AV and RSV *work*).

Difficulty has been found in the final word *there* (Heb. *šām*). Gordis maintains that the expression is satirical: 'There is a proper time for everything and every deed – over there!' citing the same word in Job 1:21; 3:17, 19 which he says refers to 'the other world, the period after death'. However, the passage contains no hint of satire. In Job 1:21 'there' refers back to 'his mother's womb'. Equally in Job 3:17, 19 the context provides a meaning to the word. Our passage is clearly of a piece with other 'orthodox' passages, such as Ecclesiastes 12:13f., which cannot all be satirical. A more usual approach is Brown, Driver and Briggs' paraphrase 'In the divine plan or scheme'. However, no parallel is cited, and they also suggest in common with many other commentators that the text might be amended to *śām* ('he has appointed' RSV).[2]

Aalders suggests that *šām* may have a weak sense without precise local force, citing Isaiah 48:16 and 2 Samuel 20:1 where the word has no clear antecedent. It then means 'there is', but not in the sense 'in that place is' (*cf.* German 'es gibt' with 'da ist', Koinē Greek *esti* with *ekei esti*). In 2 Samuel 20:1 the word still seems to have a local force, although the antecedent is not

---

[1] See further, pp. 145-146.   [2] BDB, p. 1027.

clear. Perhaps it arises out of the use of source material. Isaiah 48:16 is more helpful. God speaks of his plan to deliver Israel from Babylonian bondage. The guarantee of its coming to pass is that God has been overseeing his purpose at all stages. 'From the time it came to be I have been there.' *Šām* has not so much a weak force as the sense 'in those circumstances', 'in those events'. So here in v.17 the meaning is 'with reference to those events': in the midst of the wicked and unjust acts of men, God is judicially at work.

18. After a straightforward beginning, *I said in my heart with regard to the sons of men...* (RSV), the Hebrew becomes difficult. Probably it should continue: 'that God is making it clear to them so that they may see that they – they by themselves – are animals'. (See Additional Note for linguistic details.)

I said in my heart: he now reflects on God's purpose in its present continuance. Even the evil actions of men may unwillingly and unknowingly fulfil the purpose of God (*cf.* Acts 2:23 for the greatest example). Equally he maintains that the injustice of men fulfils at least one aspect of the purpose of God: it provides a massive demonstration on the stage of history of our ignorance regarding our own nature and destiny. God is not indifferent to injustice (v. 17); for the present it is an 'under the sun' monstrosity which reveals the essential character of fallen man (7:29). If this appears to be hard cynicism, it must be noted that the Preacher is careful to include the emphatic phrase 'they by themselves'. If, however, we lapse from the viewpoint of faith, the one element which distinguishes us from the animals is lost. Man *by himself* becomes a 'naked ape'.

Additional Note on the translation of Ecclesiastes 3:18

This verse may be translated: '...that God is making it clear to them so that they may see that they – they by themselves – are animals.' This rests on the following exegetical observations:

(i) *'al diḇraṯ* may be translated 'with respect to, concerning' (*cf.* Ec. 7:14; 8:2). In Psalm 110:4 the expression has a different force.

(ii) *lᵉḇārām* is apparently the infinitive construct of *bārar* with prefix *l* and suffix (Gordis views it as the perfect of *bārar* with asseverative *l*; this may claim other Semitic parallels but the translation is not greatly affected). The meaning of *bārar* in the Old Testament is generally 'to purify, to select'. In this passage, however, the meaning 'to make clear', more commonly found in late Hebrew, makes better sense.[1]

(iii) The suffix *-ām* refers back to *bᵉnē ha'ā-ḏām*. *Hā'lōhîm* is the most likely subject. The construction is that of a verb of saying followed by *lāmeḏ* and the infinitive to express indirect speech. *Cf.* 1 Kings 19:4, *wayyišᵉ'al eṯ-napšō āmûṯ*, Elijah 'asked that his life might die'.

(iv) The word *lir'ōṯ* may be taken as infinitive construct with prefix *lāmeḏ* to express purpose as in Genesis 11:5. Unlike that instance, however, the usage involves a change of subject, '…that God is making it clear to them that *they* might see…'. This is not without parallel. In 2 Samuel 12:10 we find, 'you have taken the wife of Uriah to be [*i.e.* that *she* may be] your wife'.[2]

(v) The phrase *šᵉhem-bᵉhēmāh hēmmāh lāhem* uses the emphatic *lāmeḏ*. The use of the *lāmeḏ* in Genesis 9:10; 23:10; Exodus 27:3, 19; Ezekiel 44:9 in each case seems to emphasize the noun to which it is attached. If, as is probable, the present case is similar, it means 'they themselves', or 'they in themselves'.[3] The generic singular *bᵉhēmāh* is best translated by an English plural. Gordis compares Psalm 90:10 and claims that *bêth* and *lāmeḏ* are interchangeable in the expression (*cf.* Ec. 2:24; 3:12; Is. 5:4).

19. The next three verses explain v.18. There is both similarity (vv.19f.) and unappreciated dissimilarity (v.21) between men and animals. Both will die; in that sense *there is no advantage of man over beast*. Their common origin is the dust of the ground (*cf.* Gn. 2:7ff.); both are fruitful and multiply (Gn. 1:22, 28; 2:7); the loss of the 'breath of life' marks the end of their earthly existence. *That which befalleth* (AV, better than RSV, NIV *fate*) refers to death. The *breath* is the breath of life, the animating principle of both men and animals. The word recurs in v.21 where it is translated 'spirit'. The common English translations imply a small change in the pointing of MT, *miqrēh* instead of *miqreh*. The MT could be translated 'The sons of men are a plaything of fate…' (so Allgeier, according to Aalders; *cf.* NEB). The interpretation above adopts the emendation of the vowel-point. The Preacher's original would have had no pointing at all.

20. The *one place* is Sheol, the realm of the dead. That we are made from the material that constitutes the world in general

---

[1] *Cf. DTTML, s.v.* [2] *Cf.* also GK 114(g).
[3] *Cf.* F. Nötscher, 'Zum Emphatischen Lamed', *VT*, 3, 1953, pp. 372–380; W. Wright, *A Grammar of the Arabic Language* (1896), pp. 41–43.

contributes to our frailty. *Dust* and *breath* (v.19; *cf*. Ps. 104:29) are not a stable combination!

21. This is best translated: 'Who knows the spirit of man *which* goes upward, and the spirit of the beast *which* goes down to the earth?' (AV, RV mg, Berkeley, NASV; the reasons for dissenting from RV, RSV, NIV are given in an additional note). The thought is twofold. First, there is a difference between man and beast in what follows death. Second, the generality of men cannot appreciate the difference in ultimate destiny and live as though there were no difference. The passage echoes Psalm 49, where man and beast are alike in dying (1–12), but distinct in their destiny beyond the grave (13–20; RSV follows an amended text and obscures the difference).[1] Likewise in Psalm 73, until the problem of injustice was faced with the perspective of 'their end' which is 'ruin' (17f.), the psalmist was 'like a beast' (22).

The complaint *Who ...?* here indicates despair (*cf*. Nu. 24:23), a concern that something is well-nigh impossible (*cf*. 1 Sa. 6:20). It is the language of generalization. The Preacher himself maintains a distinction between the ultimate destinies of men and animals (12:7), but the vast majority seem unaware of the fact. Thus interpreted the passage follows in the traditional approach to injustice in Israelite wisdom literature: the unjust are set 'in slippery places', yet fail to 'consider their end' (Ps. 73:17f.)

To *go down to the earth* appears to mean 'cease to be effective'. A similar idiom is used in 1 Samuel 3:19. In this context is seems to indicate that the governing principle of life ceases entirely. Man's breath, however, *goes upward*. Precisely how life after death is conceived is not elucidated. We are merely told that God takes human life in a different manner from that of the animal. Since the Preacher uses the concept 'above' for the sovereignty and majesty of God (*cf*. on 5:2), the phrase probably says simply that human life subsequent to death is dealt with by God.

The spirit of man may be viewed from three interrelated aspects: (i) It is the principle of life within. In this sense both men and animals have 'breath of life' from God. It does not 'dwell in man for ever', a fact that sets a limit to human life (Gn. 6:3). The origin of this 'spirit', to the Preacher's mind, is clouded in mystery (11:5). (ii) It is also the principle of human resolution, vigour, thought and moral energy. Thus, to lose one's drive or courage is for the 'spirit' to depart (Jos. 5:1). Its close relation to

[1] See J. A. Motyer, *After Death* (1965), pp. 22f.

intelligence and understanding is seen in Job 32:8: 'There is a spirit (*rûaḥ*) in man, and the breath (*nᵉšāmāh*) of the Almighty gives understanding.' Thus it is the instrument of reflection (Ps. 77:6) and of questing for God (Is. 26:9). (iii) It is also one's dominant disposition, frame of mind, emotional state, character; Caleb stood out from his contemporaries because he 'had another spirit within him' (Nu. 14:24). Thus human 'breath' differs from that of the animals not only in the afterlife, but also because it involves so much more in the present.

Additional Note on the translation of Ecclesiastes 3:21

Since the translation as a question in indirect speech ('Who knows... whether...?') is widely accepted, it is worth stating the objections to it more fully.

MT *hāʿōlāh* and *hayyōreḏeṯ* mean 'which goes up' and 'which goes down'. Following the LXX, however, it is frequently read as *haʿōlāh* and *hᵃyōreḏeṯ* which means 'whether it goes up' and 'whether it goes down'. On the former view it indicates that men do not appreciate the truth about life after death; on the latter pointing, the Preacher is querying life after death. No major point of interpretation is affected, for if the question were entirely sceptical it would simply express the common 'under the sun' viewpoint of unjust men. It would then contain the thought later expressed in 8:11 and would be corrected by the later reflection of 12:7.

There are good reasons, however, for preferring the MT as it stands and seeing the verse in harmony with 12:7, implying a difference between the destinies of men and animals. In common Hebrew idiom, if the sentence were a question in indirect speech, the interrogative *hē* would not come so late in the sentence. One would expect *mî yōḏēaʿ ᵃrûᵃḥ*... It is precisely this construction that is found in 2:19 but not here (*cf.* Gn. 8:8; 24:21, 23; 37:32, *etc.*). The construction with the participle and article is common-place (*cf.* Gn. 13:5; Jdg. 16:24; 1 Sa. 1:26). A. B. Davidson cites many examples.[1] There seems to be no sentence in the Hebrew Old Testament where the interrogative *hē* is found so late in the sentence as would be the case if an interrogative *hē* were found here. To disregard this fact and continue to treat the verse as containing a question in indirect speech is surely unwarranted.

[1] *Cf.* DS 22 R.4.

Aalders also urges that if the *h* were interrogative we would expect an indicative verb rather than a participle. This seems to be borne out by other instances of 'Who knows...?' followed by an indicative verb in Joel 2:14 and Jonah 3:9.

22. If God is sovereign in his disposal of earthly events (3:1–15), has a purpose even in allowing human injustices (3:16–20), and holds our ultimate destiny in his hands (21), then the attitude of the wise should be joyful confidence in the pursuit of earthly responsibilities and the pleasures they bring. *Portion* (AV) or *lot* (RSV) carries the idea of a share in good things (*cf.* Gn. 31:14). God intends the wise man to enjoy earthly blessings, including work, food and drink (5:18), wealth and possessions (5:19) and family joys (9:9). *Who...after him?* refers, as the parallel in 6:12 with its *under the sun* shows, not to judgment and the hereafter, but to the earthly events in which one has no part after one's death.

II. Life 'under the sun' (4:1 – 10:20)

From this point it is not easy to trace a clear consecutive argument. Later on (11:1 – 12:8) a note of exhortation breaks in, moving the argument forward again. Between 4:1 and 10:20 Ecclesiastes resembles the book of Proverbs, with short epigrams dealing with various aspects of life. Groups of sayings, however, can be seen clustered around particular themes. Every unit between 5:8 and 6:12 deals in some way with wealth; each unit of 4:1–16 bears on the need of companionship; chs. 9:13 – 10:20 directly consider the limits of wisdom and the various manifestations of folly. The book bears evidence, therefore, of structure and arrangement, although it is at times difficult to discern. It is also conspicuous that the presuppositions in 1:2 – 3:22 continue to underlie each theme taken up. The vanity of life 'under the sun' comes in for heavy fire; the life of faith in a sovereign God is urged from time to time as the only remedy.

It is best, therefore, to treat the middle section of Ecclesiastes as a guide to life 'under the sun', presenting a series of major issues, each in turn from the viewpoint of the 'under the sun' limitation and from the viewpoint of faith. The Preacher faces the big issues: the hardships of life and the companionship it demands, poverty and wealth, the vexations of circumstances and of man himself, the authority of kings and authority misapplied, the limits of wisdom and the encroachments of folly. 'Look!' he says in effect. 'This is what it is really like. Can you face life in this world as it really is? There is only one way to do so.' The various themes overlap considerably, so that several topics are considered more than once from different angles.

A. LIFE'S HARDSHIPS AND LIFE'S COMPANIONS (4:1 – 5:7)

The dominant note in this section is the need of companionship. Successive units deal with oppression without comforters (*And I saw...*, 4:1–3), work that is lonely (*Then I saw...*, 4:4–6), a man without the companionship of family (*Again, I saw...*, 4:7f.), followed by proverbs on the need of companionship (4:9–12).

Then comes a brief glimpse of a lonely king (4:13–16). This leaves a section (5:1–7) which seems to belong neither to ch. 4 nor to 5:8–6:12 (which has its own unity). Perhaps the viewpoint of faith is again being brought in: there is a God in heaven opposed to earthly injustice and loneliness, the God of Israel, who is worshipped at the temple of Jerusalem.

i. Oppression without comfort (4:1–3). 1. Although similar to 3:16–22, this unit is a fresh reflection (AV *I returned*; RSV *again*). The Preacher is an eyewitness (*I saw*) of life's oppressions. No particular era is in mind (*pace* Leupold); injustice characterizes life as a whole. It is evil 'under the sun', not under the aegis of any particular ruler (v.3).

It is not expected that oppressions will be borne with stoical silence. Grief-stricken Israelites were never inhibited from shedding *tears*, as psalmists, apostles and their colleagues, and our Lord himself bear witness (Ps. 119:136; Jn. 11:35; Acts 8:2).

Compassion for the *oppressed* is common in the Old Testament. Oppression of people by a king (Pr. 28:16), of a servant by his master (Dt. 24:14), of the poor by the affluent (Pr. 22:16; Am. 4:1), the bureaucratic (Ec. 5:8) or even by others who are poor (Pr. 28:3), is viewed with indignation. The temporary resident, the alien, the fatherless and the widow receive especial sympathy (Je. 7:6; Ezk. 22:7; Zc. 7:10). High interest rates (Ezk. 22:12, 29), corrupt weights and measures (Ho. 12:7) and oppressive estate agents (Mi. 2:2) are among oppressions singled out for rebuke.

It is particularly embittering that *oppressors* should have *power* at all. The Hebrew of the latter part of the verse reads: 'From/in the hand of the oppressor, power.' This has been taken to mean (i) 'From the hands of the oppressors *went forth* power' (Barton), or (ii) '…went forth violence', or (iii) 'In the hand of the oppressor is power'. The first reads too much into the text; the second gives an unusual meaning to the Hebrew *kōᵃḥ* (strength); the last is most likely (*cf.* RSV). Aalders points to the similarity of *miyyad* ('in the hand of') to *miṣṣad* ('on the side of', *cf.* 1 Sa. 20:25).[1] The repetition of *there is no comforter* heightens the sense of helplessness. What is lacking, in fact, is actual 'comfort'. Job's 'comforters' failed to provide it (Jb. 16:2). The point here is similar: earthly resources give no relief.

[1] It makes no difference to the sense whether *oppressions…oppressed* (RSV) is the translation or (as is possible since the same Hebrew word is used) 'oppressed… oppressed' (so Ginsburg, Leupold).

2. This bitter verdict contrasts starkly with 2:26 and 3:22, which deal with life received from the hand of God. Here the Preacher presses the logic of the restricted 'under the sun' viewpoint. God-less sorrow leads to suicidal longings (*cf.* Mt. 27:5; 2 Cor. 7:10). The horizontal view of life has no 'smile beneath the tyrant's frown' (contrast Ps. 119:50; Is. 25:8).

3. Better still is never to have lived, to have been unaware of life's vanity. Again there is no attempt at a solution (*cf.* 6:3–5; Je. 20:18). The same point is made in Herodotus, Theognis, Sophocles, Cicero (*cf.* Barton) and Buddhism (*cf.* Plumptre), testimony to the widespread consciousness of the problem rather than an indication of literary relationships.

ii. Lonesome rivalry and its alternatives (4:4–6). **4.** The Preacher sees that the main motivation for work is human rivalry. Effort put forth (*toil*) and success in techniques acquired (*skill*) often hide the scramble for wealth, leadership, power or status. The ancient world too had its international tensions, labour disputes and class conflict. Beneath the surface of human energies the Preacher sees the restless desire to outclass others. Elsewhere the wisdom writers describe the destructive influences of *envy* which 'enrages' a man and makes him harsh (Pr. 6:34) and destroys him physically (Pr. 14:30). This is one more depressing aspect of life 'under the sun' for it means man's efforts are damaged at every stage. If his toil originates in ambition (4:4), if its progress is liable to be inhibited by folly (2:19, 21), if its results may be nil (1:3; 5:15), any hope of gain can come only from God (3:13; 5:18f.). Admittedly the Preacher is generalizing, and a different perspective will come later (9:10); but the fullest outlook is reserved for later days (*cf.* 1 Cor. 10:31; Eph. 6:5–8; Col. 3:22f.).

If 4:1–16 is indeed a string of units edited around the theme of companionship, the underlying concern will be the social fragmentation produced by such toil. Rivalry never produced companionship yet. The precise thought is not that work *causes* rivalry (Berkeley), but that it *stems from* rivalry. The Hebrew means 'envy towards one's neighbour' (*cf.* RSV) rather than 'envy from one's neighbour' (*cf.* AV, RV) or between 'man and man' (*cf.* Moffatt, NEB, JB).[1]

---

[1] The Hebrew term may be followed by the accusative (Nu. 5:14), by the preposition *bêṭ* (Gn. 30:1) or *lameḏ* (Ps. 106:16). For it to be followed by *min*

5. This is the opposite of v.4. We pass from the rat-race with its hectic scramble for status symbols to the drop-out with his total indifference. His condition is analysed as self-cannibalism, he *consumes his own flesh*. To *fold the hands* is to be idle (*cf.* Pr. 6:10).

6. The *handful of quietness* is the middle way between the clamourous grasping of v.4 and the escapism of v.5. The two words for *hand* differ in the Hebrew; the second refers to hands cupped to take as much as possible (*cf.* Ex. 9:8). The way of wisdom will attempt much (*one handful*) but not too much (*two hands full*), and so will find life within its grasp (*one handful*) not an impossible strain (*striving for wind*). How such a life is attained is the underlying theme of Ecclesiastes. It is 'from the hand of God' (2:24), 'a gift' (5:19). A fuller exposition comes in 9:7–10; 11:1–10. Its embodiment is seen in Christ who withdrew from 'two hands full' of trouble (Mt. 12:14f.), but was noted for his 'handful of quietness' (Mt. 12:19f.).

iii. A man without a family (4:7–8).

A picture is presented of a man who has neither friend (av *a second*; niv *all alone*) nor close relative (*son...brother*) for company. His achievements, although profitable (*riches* result), do not satisfy. A companion or heir might be appreciative, but none is available. This is part of life's *futility*, an appointed *travail* (*cf.* 1:13) which cannot be escaped.

For whom am I working...? comes in abruptly (rsv *so that he never asks* is not in the original). The Preacher puts himself in the shoes of the lonely man. nab gives the sense by putting the question in inverted commas: '*For whom do I toil...?*'[1]; neb *he asks* (*cf.* niv) has the same effect. The point is not that he never asks the question (av, rsv), but that he finds no answer.[2]

Thus again the question of life's purpose is raised. A man without companions or family will act as though there were someone to live for (*cf.* Ps. 39:6). But for whom? On secular premises (*under the sun*, v.7) there is no answer. Although it is beyond the horizon of Ecclesiastes, Ambrose and Jerome were

---

indicating the object of jealousy is not found elsewhere, but it is parallel to *fear* followed by Hebrew *min* in Lv. 19:14, 32; Ec. 12:5 (*cf.* Gordis).

[1] This is an instance where R. Gordis' theory of unannounced quotations is convincing (*cf.* 'Quotations: as a Literary Usage in Biblical, Oriental and Rabbinic Literature', *HUCA*, 22, 1949, pp. 157–219); other instances are not so convincing.

[2] gnb changes *I* in this verse to *he*, but without textual warrant.

not so wrong in suggesting that the missing companion is Christ (*cf.* Ginsburg).

iv. The blessings of companionship (4:9–12). A partial solution to the sorrows of the lonely is found in the blessings of companionship. The central point made in v.9 is expounded in vv.10–12a with three illustrations; v.12b extends the principle further. Possibly all three illustrations are taken from the risks of travel: pits and ravines along the way (10), cold nights (11) and wayside marauders (12a). They highlight the blessings of companionship in error or mishap (10), adversity (11) or hostility (12a).

9. *Toil* is very unspecific; whatever responsibilities or pursuits may be undertaken, companionship will help surmount the difficulties. *Reward* (*śākār*) often means 'wages', but a more general usage is found (Gn. 15:1; 2 Ch. 15:7; Ps. 127:3); here it refers to the success that comes through co-operation.

10. A fall into a ditch or pit (*cf.* Gn. 14:10; Lk. 6:39) is the background to the first illustration. A lonely fall might be fatal, especially at night. The proverb, however, looks beyond physical mishap; slips of judgment and other types of 'falling by the wayside' equally need a helping hand. The Hebrew is strictly plural ('If they fall…'), but occasionally the plural may 'denote an indefinite singular'[1] and thus mean 'If either of them should fall…'.

11. This may allude to husband and wife, but travellers in Israel's cold winter nights (*cf.* Je. 36:22, 30) slept close together. The proverb speaks of companionship in adversity, temptation or grief.

12. A third illustration is taken from the burglar or wayside bandit. The lonely traveller may be overcome; safety is found in numbers.[2] The strength of the three-ply cord was proverbial in the ancient world, as seen in Sumerian and Akkadian texts.[3] The numerical sequence x, x+1, is fairly common in the Old Testament (*cf.* Ec. 11:2; Am. 1:3, *etc.*) and generally indicates a

[1] GK 124(e).
[2] Gordis and Delitzsch think that the verb means 'attack' rather than 'overcome'. GNB seems to agree. This is doubtful, but in any case the meaning is not greatly affected. The unusual Hebrew has led to numerous speculative emendations of *ytqrw*. Ellermeier (pp. 174–177) lists the main ones.
[3] *Cf.* A. Schaffer, 'New Light on the Three-Ply Cord', in A. Malamat, *Eretz-Israel*, vol. 9 (1969), pp. 139, 159–160.

full measure of what is being referred to.[1] The move from two or three may, therefore, be a hint that there is nothing sacrosanct about the pair and that companionship may operate within larger numbers. Gordis sees here a reference to a son being born to a married couple. In some realms progress may be measured by increasing independence; in this realm spiritual stature is measured by growing interdependence.

v. Isolation breeding folly (4:13–16). 13. The next unit has links with the themes of isolation (4:7f.) and companionship (4:9–12), for v.13 continues to underline the folly of self-sufficiency and growing isolation. Attempts have been made to identify the characters of these verses, but none is entirely convincing.[2] The scene is too commonplace.

Generally in the Old Testament wisdom is reckoned to lie with increasing age and experience, and the elderly were honoured accordingly (Lv. 19:32). But it is also realized that the aged may lose their wisdom (Jb. 12:20) and that the young may be wiser than their elders (Ps. 119:100). Elihu's is the balanced position, giving his elders the first hearing but not regarding them as infallible, since the Spirit of God may give wisdom beyond one's years (Jb. 32:4–11).

The Preacher applies the same point to an unnamed, probably hypothetical, king. He once (*no longer*) listened to advice, but now is growingly isolated as he becomes 'wise in his own eyes' (Pr. 26:12). The whole process is unconscious, as implied by the phrase *no longer knows* (NIV; the reference to knowing is omitted in RSV, NEB).

In this situation a *youth* of humble origins[3] may outstrip him. The word is not 'teenager' but 'young man', for it takes in Joseph at seventeen years (Gn. 37:30) and Rehoboam's advisers who were over forty (1 Ki. 12:8; 14:21). AV *child* is misleading.

---

[1] *Cf.* comments on Ec. 11:2, and references cited.

[2] Eight possibilities are listed by Gordis. See also K. D. Schunk, 'Drei Seleukiden im Buche Kohelet', *VT*, 9, 1959, pp. 192–201; W. A. Irwin, 'Eccles. 4, 13–16', *JNES*, 3, 1944, pp. 255–257; Ellermeier, pp. 217–232. C. C. Torrey ('The Problem of Ecclesiastes IV 13–16', *VT*, 2, 1952, pp. 175–177) suggests it is displaced from Ec. 10:16–17, but there is no evidence that such is the case.

[3] E. A. Speiser translates *miskēn* 'underprivileged' and compares the *muskenum*, 'the "state's dependents" who assumed certain onerous obligations and restrictions in return for fief-holdings', in the laws of Hammurabi and the Mari documents (*Oriental and Biblical Studies* (1967), pp. 332–345, esp. p. 343). *Cf.* also CPIQ, p. 206.

GNB merges the staccato proverbs of vv.13f. into one lengthy sentence and lapses from accuracy altogether in v.15.

14. The obscurities of this verse revolve around the ambiguity of *he*. One way of taking it is: *For he* (the young man) *has come out of prison*[1] *to become king, even though he* (the young man) *was born poor in his* (the older king's) *kingdom* (following NASV). This seems likely (following Gordis and Aalders), for then the *poor* man of v.14 is the same *poor yet wise* man of v.13, and the king implicit in *kingdom* is the same king as in v.13. In ambiguities of this nature it seems best to have the key-words retaining a consistent meaning.[2] Interpreted thus, the verse tells more about the young man's humble origin: he had everything against him, only wisdom helped him to the throne.

15. This may be translated: 'I have seen all the living under the sun throng to the side of the second, the lad who replaces him' (NIV is similar). *Second youth* has caused some difficulty. Some take it to refer to another character, a second youth who, when the first youth becomes old, repeats the process all over again (so, tentatively, Barton). Others feel this is impossibly complex and delete *second* as a gloss. A third approach, although the Hebrew is unusual, takes the old king as the 'first' and the youth as the 'second' and translates as above, 'the second, the youth'. The first interpretation makes the paragraph needlessly complex; the second is without textual evidence; the third is the most satisfactory.

16. *There was* (or 'is') *no end to all the people* (NIV) is followed by an appositional phrase 'all before whom he was'. It is a difficult expression, but Ginsburg points to the phrase 'to go out and in before' meaning to 'lead' (*cf.* Nu. 27:17). So Leupold's 'those that constituted his followers' catches the thought.[3] Despite the large following the young king received, it was not lasting. People are fickle and may cast their palms before a new arrival, only to cry 'Crucify him!' a few days later.

The final phrase sums up the Preacher's point. The little tale is more evidence of the *vanity* of our world, and of the frustration

---

[1] For Barton's view that we have here a reference to a 'house of the rebellious' (a hostile dynasty), *cf.* Gordis and GK 35(d) who show that *prison* is correct.

[2] Thus *he…he* is the young man; others take the first *he* to be the young man and the second as the king (so Levy, according to Gordis), or both as the king (so Kidner).

[3] Gordis and NASV take the phrase to refer to previous generations, *all who were before them*.

that comes of trying to make sense of it. Within the last four verses we have seen another form of growing isolation without companionship, that of a king who grows too self-confident and feels he needs no advisers. He falls from favour and a new regime takes over. Despite his humble origins, the crowd flocks to the side of the newcomer who too will grow old and be abandoned in turn to his own isolation.

vi. The approach to God (5:1–7).[1] Earth's 'vanity' has been recognized (1:2 – 2:23), but considered in the light of the life God gives (2:24–26) and the assurance of his sovereignty (3:1–15). Injustice (3:16–22) and various forms of isolation (4:1–16) have been faced. We stand in need of an altogether greater companionship. The Preacher earlier told of a God who gives a life of joy and pleasure. May he be approached? This question is now answered in terms of the house of God, obedience, sacrifice (v.1), prayer (vv.2f.), vows (v.4). But there are dangers. If God is 'in heaven', the ruler (3:1–15) and judge (3:16–22), he cannot be approached casually. So a proverbial unit is inserted dealing with our approach to God. The first note of exhortation in Ecclesiastes comes here, and assumes God may be approached, addressed in prayer, and will receive our vows.

1. The *house of God* (GNB *temple*) may refer to any place where God reveals himself (*cf.* Gn. 28:17, 22), including the tabernacle (Ex. 23:19, *etc.*) or other Israelite sanctuaries (*cf.* Jdg. 18:31). Pagan shrines were also 'houses' of the deity concerned (Jdg. 9:27; 1 Sa. 5:5). Here the reference is to Solomon's temple built in the tenth century BC and destroyed in 587 BC, or (on a post-exilic dating of Ecclesiastes) to the second temple built in 520–516 BC, destroyed by the Romans in 63 BC, rebuilt and enlarged by Herod the Great in 19 BC. Despite major devastations, it maintained its symbolic structure, highlighting the holiness of God and his inaccessibility except by propitiatory sacrifices. To the godly Israelite it was the focal point of reverent devotion and meditation; he loved it for the divine glory which was there, in which he desired to dwell 'for ever'.

Guard your feet (Heb.) refers to demeanour and preparedness as one comes to worship, particularly readiness to obey, for *listen*

---

[1] The versification of the Hebrew Old Testament and the English versions diverges here. Ecclesiastes 5:1–20 in the English versions represents 4:17 – 5:19 in the Hebrew text.

refers to heeding as well as hearing (*cf.* Lk. 8:18). The second half of the comparison is literally '…than that fools should give a sacrifice (*zebah*)'. The *zebah* was an offering killed in sacrifice and then used for a meal, in contrast to the whole burnt-offering (*'ōlâ*) which was totally consumed in sacrifice. As Delitzsch points out, it is the *zebah* which could degenerate into thoughtless festivity, or worse (*cf.* Pr. 7:14). The Preacher is probably attacking not the sacrificial system, but its misuse (*cf.* 1 Sa. 15:22).[1]

Another characteristic of the *fool* (*ke sîl*) appears: 'they are ignorant in doing wrong'. The Hebrew of this last phrase is difficult; it literally reads 'they do not know to do evil'. Ginsburg takes it to mean that 'they (who obey) know not how to do evil', but the subject seems to be the fool. Barton reads 'they do not know *except* to do evil', but it is unlikely that there is any ellipsis of 'except'. More likely the last clause is one of result ('…and so they do wrong', Leupold), of time ('…when they do wrong', Berkeley), or of attendant circumstances ('…in doing wrong'); the difference is small, the last is the best attested grammatically.[2]

2. For the Preacher hastiness of spirit is always a mistake (7:9); here he warns against it in prayer. Ill-considered words may pour out in anguish (Jb. 40:3–5) or in resentment (Ps. 73:15). Careless words are a reflection of the inner life; for it is the *heart*[3] that speaks forth a *word* (*cf.* Moffatt *Never let your heart hurry you into words*, and AV, RV, RSV. *Heart* is lost in several other translations). *Before God* shows the temple is still in mind (*cf.* Is. 37:14).

Heaven may be used of the sky conceived visually (*cf.* Ps. 8:3 and the Heb. of Ec. 10:20) or of the cosmos other than the earth (Gn. 1:1). Here it is the dwelling-place of God, sometimes called the 'height of heaven' or the 'heaven of heavens' (Jb. 22:12; 1 Ki. 8:27). This does not imply his absence from earth, for elsewhere it is said that he is 'in heaven above *and* on the earth below' (Dt. 4:39). Rather *heaven* is a reminder of his greatness; it is the location of his glory. Thus our impatience with God is rebuked by God's greatness compared to man's smallness. Mankind must always be a suppliant, never an equal. To

---

[1] *Cf.* W. B. Stevenson, 'Hebrew 'Olah and Zebach Sacrifices', *Festschrift für Alfred Bertholet* (1950).

[2] For clauses with *lamed* and infinitive denoting attendant circumstances ('when they do wrong', 'in doing wrong'), *cf.* GK 114(e).

[3] See p. 62.

restrain the tongue is the Preacher's way of wisdom. The point was later embodied in the Lord's Prayer, where the twin truths that God is 'Father' but 'in heaven' guard against craven fear on the one hand and flippancy on the other.

3. The explanatory *For* links the thought to the previous verse. What may cause impatience in prayer is a *multitude of business*. Heavy responsibility is apt to hinder concentration and lead to impatience in prayer. The *fool* will consequently pour out a flood of words, but this is no remedy. The need for care in prayer cannot be set aside. Acts 4:24–31 provides a classic illustration with its worship (24) and application of Scripture (25–28), before its single request (29f.) and its dramatic result (31). AV *is known* is an unnecessary insertion. NEB loses all reference to a dream, apparently amending *haḥᵃlôm* (the *dream*) to a hypothetical *heḥālûm*, translated 'the sensible man' but unattested elsewhere.

4. The Preacher moves to vows paid in the temple (4–7). The *vow* in ancient Israel was a promise to God, which might be part of prayer for blessing (Nu. 21:2) or a spontaneous expression of gratitude (Jon. 2:9). It might take the form of a promise of allegiance (Gn. 28:20–22), a free-will offering (Lv. 22:18) or the dedication of a child as Nazirite (1 Sa. 1:11). As in the matter of prayer, haste in taking a vow is cautioned against elsewhere (Pr. 20:25). Here the Preacher warns against *delay* (*cf.* Dt. 23:21–23) and evasion: *Pay what you vow!* Failure in these respects is a mark of *fools*.

5. Because the vow was voluntary, there was danger of its becoming a form of bribery, especially in times of distress.

6. God does not take broken vows lightly.[1] A broken vow may incur his judgment upon our endeavours. One who 'swears to his own hurt and does not change' pleases God (Ps. 15:4). Thus the *mouth* may lead the *flesh* into sin. *Flesh* here apparently refers to the whole man, hence RSV ... *lead you into sin*.[2] It is possible that it also stresses moral frailty, a point which becomes more explicit in its New Testament usage (*cf.* Gal. 5:16–21) but is rare in the Old Testament.

---

[1] In Ec. 5:6 it is a sacrifice at the temple that is in mind. The Preacher does not deal with a vow which was downright sinful in the first place; that is a matter for repentance rather than fulfilment.

[2] R. B. Salters maintains that 'The idea here is that something small, *i.e.* the mouth, may bring guilt upon the whole, *i.e.* the entire person' (*cf.* Jas. 3:5). So 'Notes on the History of the Interpretation of Koh 5 5', *ZATW*, 90, 1978, pp. 95–101.

Hebrew draws no distinction between *messenger* and *angel*, so several interpretations are open to us here. Does the verse refer to (i) the angel of the LORD who is called in the Old Testament 'a man' or 'an angel' but is addressed as divine? Or (ii) to a prophet (Hg. 1:13; Mal. 3:1); or (iii) to a priest (Mal. 2:7); or (iv) to a messenger sent by a priest? One of the last two is almost certainly correct. A voluntary offering vowed to a temple priest is unfulfilled; the temple priest or his messenger[1] comes to enquire. 'Oh, *it was a mistake*' is the worshipper's evasion. But God sees, and a careless approach to him may bring his anger upon our words and his judgment upon our works, if not immediately (*cf.* 8:11) at least ultimately (12:14).

7. The Hebrew of the earlier part of this verse is difficult. NAB and NEB omit it altogether. As it stands the Hebrew text may be translated: (i) 'For in many dreams and vanities, there are also many words...' (Delitzsch); (ii) 'For just as there are dreams in abundance, so there are also vain words in abundance' (Aalders);[2] (iii) 'In spite of many dreams and vanities and words, fear God!' (Gordis).[3] On any view it makes the same point: people are prone to carry their illusions with them while they worship and also to talk without thinking. If a vow is made this way, the worshipper is treading on dangerous ground. The remedy is to *fear God*.[4]

B. POVERTY AND WEALTH (5:8 – 6:12)

The various proverbs of this section are bound together by the theme of poverty and wealth. We have reference to 'the poor' (5:8), 'money' (5:10), the increase of 'good things' (5:11), the 'rich man' (5:12), 'riches' (5:13–14), 'riches and wealth' (5:19; 6:2), the 'poor man' (6:8).

i. The poor under oppressive bureaucracy (5:8–9). First the

---

[1] 'Messenger of Milk-'Aštart' and 'priest of Milk-'Aštart' are found in Phoenician inscriptions as possible synonyms. *Cf.* CPIQ, p. 207. Dahood argues that the 'messenger' was a religious functionary sent out from Jerusalem by the temple priest to outlying communities.

[2] This involves taking $b^e r \bar{o} b$ as a separate phrase in the absolute state, treating the second w^e as a comparison, and taking *vanities and words* as a hendiadys.

[3] This involves a rare use of b^e as 'in spite of'.

[4] For comment on the fear of God, see pp. 82, 122–123.

Preacher considers the frustrations of oppressive bureaucracy with its endless delays and excuses, while the poor cannot afford to wait, and justice is lost between the tiers of the hierarchy. At this point the Preacher offers no remedy; this is what human nature is like.

8. The meaning of *province* (RSV) or *district* (NIV) will depend on the date given to Ecclesiastes (see comments on 2:8). The explanation (*For...*) has been taken to refer to suspicious rivalry between officials (*one official preying on another*, Moffatt). This, however, is scarcely an explanation, although a hostile meaning to the verb is found in 1 Samuel 19:11 and Psalm 56:6, nor do AV and RV give a good rendering; the translation required by the context is 'One official looks after the interests of another' (*cf.* GNB). The final phrase, *and there are high-ups over them*, refers to the successive tiers of authority. This is preferable to taking the plural as one of majesty referring to the king (NEB) or to the overriding providence of God (NEB mg.).

9. The beginning of the verse may be translated: *And an advantage to* (or *for*, or *of*) *a land is....* Then the Hebrew becomes difficult. Should it be translated 'for all' (AV, JB), 'in all' (RSV), 'on the whole' (Barton, Leupold), 'over everything' (Gordis), 'after all' (NASV, Moffatt) or 'always' (Delitzsch)? Is the word 'served' (Heb. *ne"ḇāḏ*) to be attached to 'king' or (as the Massoretic pointing suggests) to 'land', and does it have a simple adjectival sense ('served', 'cultivated') or a permissive sense ('allowed to be cultivated')?[1] This in turn leads to numerous possibilities of translation. Is the advantage 'a king whose own lands are well tilled' (NEB)? Or that 'even a king is subject to the soil' (Gordis; *cf.* AV)? Or is the advantage 'a king for a field under tillage' (Plumptre)? Or 'a king who has control' (Moffatt)? Or 'that a cultivated land has a king' (as a counterweight to bureaucratic corruption; so Lauha, *cf.* also Barton)? In context the main point must be that bureaucratic officialdom does not totally override the value of kingly authority. A likely translation is therefore: 'But an advantage to a land for everyone is: a king over cultivated land.' This understands the 'all' to refer back to the poor, the officials and the higher officials of v.8; hence 'for everyone'. It is also possible to take 'land' (*śaḏeh*) to refer to a specific country (Ru. 1:1, RSV). If Aalders is right in suggesting that 'cultivated' has permissive force, then another likely trans-

[1] *Cf.* GK 51(c); Joüon 51(c).

lation is '…a king over a land which is allowed to be cultivated'. If either of these two translations is correct, the writer is sensitive to oppression (v.8) but does not hold that anarchy or violent revolution is a viable alternative.

ii. Money and its drawbacks (5:10–12). Three perennial drawbacks to wealth are crisply presented: it cannot satisfy the covetous (10); it attracts a circle of dependents (11); it disturbs one's peace (12).

10. If poverty has its problems, love of wealth is not an appropriate alternative (*cf.* Ps. 37:16). The words *money* (*keseƀ*, 'silver') and *wealth* (*hamôn*, 'abundance, plenty') are respectively silver used as a medium of exchange, and wealth in the form of goods and possessions (*cf.* Ezk. 29:19, RSV). They speak of the capital one has, while *gain* (*t^eƀû'â*, 'income, increase, harvest') is the hope of further income, a 'harvest' in store (for the word has agricultural associations).

11. In general (for wisdom literature deals in generalizations) promotion anticipated is more attractive than promotion in the event. Increased wealth brings increased taxation (in more than one sense!). For riches have a knack of disappearing down a drain of increased responsibilities. An 'extended family' will extend a bit further with each increment; the wage-earner will *see* the goods but no more.

12. A glimpse is given of two case histories. The *rich* man suffers from insomnia. Either his physique or his cares keep him awake. On the other hand a labourer, though comparatively poorer, finds that both his daily work and his freedom from care enable him to sleep soundly. The Preacher asks: whose position is preferable? The rich man's *surfeit* (RSV) has been taken to refer to his wealth (NIV, JB; *cf.* GNB *has so much*) or his *full stomach* (NASV). Translations which retain the ambiguity are best.

iii. Wealth – loved and lost (5:13–17). We now pass to those who have had wealth and lost it. First the tale is presented; we see wealth acquired (13) and lost (14a), and man's inability to pass anything on (14b) or take anything with him (15). Then follows a grim view of the life of the one who loved and lost his wealth (16f.).

13. The calamity (RSV *evil*) is painful, sickening (RSV *grievous* is *ḥōlāh*, from *ḥālāh* 'to be or become ill'). During his life this man's wealth did him no good. The reader is left to imagine the price that was paid – be it moral decadence following ill-gotten gain or physical deterioration following restless nights (*cf.* 5:12).

14. The riches were suddenly and catastrophically lost, whether in foolish gambling, in a misguided venture, or in a sudden reversal of circumstances. To add to the tragedy, a son is also drawn into it.

15. The verse does not say he takes *nothing* with him; he takes nothing *in his hand* (*i.e.* tangible, material possessions). With him go his character and his conscience.

16. The Hebrew for *just as* is emphatic and may be translated 'quite exactly as'.[1] What a man has in his hand at birth signifies what capital he brought with him – nothing. What he may take with him exactly corresponds. The accumulation was futile.

17. We see what this man's wealth cost him. *Darkness* (*cf.* 2:13–14) symbolizes his misery. Preoccupation with wealth led to a gloomy life. *Sickness* points to the physical strain. *Vexation* indicates the cares and frustrations that tore at his mind and heart. *Wrath* tells of the times he was enraged over thwarted ambitions and schemes. NIV *he eats in darkness* follows MT; RSV follows the LXX which has 'and grief' instead of 'eats' (*w'bl* for *y'kl*); MT *eats* is used in the sense of 'lives one's life' (*cf.* Am. 7:12). The cost was tragic.

iv. Remedy recalled (5:18–20). The bitterness of the life-story just sketched makes this an appropriate place for the Preacher to recall his remedy. No mention was made of God in 5:13–17; *under the sun* indicated his world-view (5:13). But the Preacher does not allow any to forget that there is another aspect to life.

18. *Behold* introduces a different angle altogether. There is another life, equally outward, real, observable. *I have seen* it, says the Preacher. It is enjoyable *in toil*, not in its absence. It is a God-given provision in a brief life. *To eat and drink* is expressive of companionship, joy and satisfaction, including religious celebration (Dt. 14:26); here it is the symbol of a contented and happy life. In 1 Kings 4:20 the phrase summarizes the peaceful contentment of Solomon's reign (*cf.* also Je. 22:15). This is the wise man's *portion* (*cf.* comment on 3:22).

19. Wealth in a secular context (for the word *God* is absent

---

[1] *Cf.* BDB, p. 769, under *'ummāh*.

throughout 5:8–17) may lead to misery. But not all wealth is thereby condemned. The possibility is held out of wealth combined with power to enjoy it. Secular-minded men may assume the two invariably go together; the Preacher regards them as distinct. The secret of such a life is God's will, for all depends on whether God gives the wealth and the power of enjoyment. On man's side it depends on acceptance of the style of life God apportions, and awareness of the God-given nature of all wealth. The Hebrew ('God…makes a master/gives mastery in order to enjoy…') suggests that a man must be in control of his attitude to wealth rather than his attitude to wealth in control of him (*cf.* Phil. 4:12).

20. Secular man may live a life of drudgery, but for the God-centred man it will be otherwise. The thought here is not that life will be so quiet that nothing memorable will take place (*pace* Leupold), but that life will be so occupied with jubilation that the vanity of life will be well-nigh forgotten. It is not entirely forgotten, however, for the word *much* (translated 'overmuch' by RSV in 7:16, a meaning suitable here) implies that life's brevity will be kept in mind (*cf.* Ps. 90:12), but not so as to give the sleepless nights of 2:23. The Hebrew of *keeps him occupied with* is linked with the term 'business' that has occurred throughout Ecclesiastes.[1] There is a business that vexes and frustrates (*cf.* 1:13; 4:8), the life given to man to live within a vain world with its kinks and gaps (*cf.* 1:15). The Preacher repeats his remedy of a God-given life of faith and joy which is even more preoccupying.

v. Wealth and its insecurity (6:1–6). A series of sketches shows the limitations of money. Wealth does not guarantee its own enjoyment (1f.); a man may live to his prime with a flourishing family but still die unsatisfied and unmourned (3). Better never to have lived than to have lived discontented (4–6a). Death is inevitable, no matter how slow in coming (6b).

1. The Preacher introduces another situation he has observed afflicting mankind. *Under the sun* again marks out the limited viewpoint. The final phrase is literally '…and great (or 'many') is it upon men'. Its similarity to 8:6 suggests that Moffatt's *that presses heavily on men* (similar to several modern translations) is

[1] The verbal form here is *ma'aneh*; the noun is *'inyan*. Both derive from *'ānāh*, 'to be busy', 'to be occupied with'. Other ways of taking the verb are considered in Gordis.

better than *is common among men* (AV). GNB *serious injustice* stretches the Hebrew.

2. The man under the blessing of God (5:18–20) has passed from view. We see instead one to whom God has given wealth, though there is no indication that he recognizes the source of his wealth. The previous man was given 'power to enjoy' what he had (5:19); this one is not, and accordingly is unable to be contented. Again the man's plight is described in general terms, leaving the reader to envisage what takes away his *power to enjoy*. Is it some calamity, or simply the playboy's boredom? He had all a man might ask for (*cf.* 2 Ch. 1:11f., echoing the same terms), but either no appetite or no opportunity to enjoy it. *Honour* adds a note unmentioned in 5:18–20; this man has fame to go with his wealth. The word (*kāḇôḏ*) need not be taken as a further term for wealth on the grounds that one can scarcely eat it (Ginsburg and others); *eat* means 'enjoy' here (*cf.* Is. 3:10). His riches do not enable him personally to achieve anything: 'a stranger may enjoy them' (as the Hebrew can be translated). He cannot even feel that at least he has passed his wealth on to a son who will fulfil his father's ambitions. The clause is a contrast (*but a stranger…*), not an explanation (*for*, NASV).

3. What if the man of 6:1f. was cut off in his prime? The Preacher takes a further example. Another man lives a long life, and has a very large family. Yet that is no guarantee of happiness, for he may die unsatisfied and unmourned. The reference to *a hundred children*, although only a generalization and an exaggeration (*cf. a thousand years*, v.6), is less extravagant than modern urbanized man might imagine (*cf.* Jdg. 8:30). RSV *lives many years, so that the days of his years are many* (*cf.* AV, RV) is needlessly repetitive. Others see here a concessive clause: 'great as may be the days of his years' (most modern translations, with Wright, Ginsburg). But Hebrew 'great' (*raḇ*) may mean 'eminent', 'great in reputation' (*cf.* La. 1:1), giving the better translation 'If a man lives many years, and is great as are the years of his life…'. The man's fame is great as his years are long.[1]

Despite family, longevity and fame, life may so miscarry as to incur lifelong dissatisfaction and an unmourned death. The *soul* in AV *his soul is not filled with good* is the whole inner 'life' of man, and is used here as his capacity for feelings, inclinations, enjoy-

---

[1] This is Aalders' view; it involves taking *še* to mean 'as' (*cf.* *'ᵃšer* in Ex. 34:18; Ps. 106:34; Is. 7:17; Je. 48:8).

ment, satisfaction. In most modern translations it is simply *he*. To die unburied was the mark of a despised and unmourned end (*cf.* Je. 22:18f. and comment on Ec. 8:10). Better to miscarry at birth than to miscarry throughout life.

4. The *child born dead* is compared in vv. 4f. with the dissatisfied rich man of v.3. *Comes* refers to its disastrous birth (*cf.* 1:4). *Into vanity* may mean 'into this vain world', but in this setting 'to no purpose' is a better translation. The *darkness* is the realm of the dead, a contrast to the realm *under the sun* (*cf.* Ps. 58:8). It would be pressing the text unduly to take it as implying misery. The *name* in Hebrew thought is more than a label; it includes the personality and the character. The still-born child has no chance to develop a character or acquire a reputation.

5. This puts negatively what v.4 said positively. The still-born child has no experience of life (*has not seen the sun*) or knowledge of this world. But the discontented rich man is worse off. The child at least has *rest*; he does not have to endure the conflicts of life 'under the sun'. Some translations lose the reference to *rest* (NASV, Moffatt, NEB; JB *never knowing rest* is an unlikely translation; it results from punctuating the Hebrew differently).

6. The question of the long life raised in v.3 is taken up. What is the use of it if it is but prolonged misery? *A thousand years twice over* is ironic exaggeration: Methuselah's life twice over cannot satisfy if the outlook is awry. The abrupt intrusion of the next comment: *Do not all go to the same place?* brushes the question of longevity aside. The destination is common to all, no matter how long it takes to get there. The *one place*[1] is 'Sheol', the realm of the dead.

vi. Insatiable longing (6:7–9). 7. The *mouth* refers to feeding; a man's labour is generally not for sheer pleasure but to earn a living. But as the treadmill goes round, his inner life with its longing for fulfilment and satisfaction is left empty. Some, seeing here only a reference to an endless need to keep alive, render it 'so that *his appetite* (or *his belly*) is never filled'. But *the longing is not satisfied* (Berkeley) sees more in the text and is surely right. 'Bread

[1] The view that the 'one place' is God himself suggested by G. Dalman and A. Spanier is rightly dismissed by P. Ackroyd. His own suggestion is that the reference is to Sheol's mouth, and Sheol's never being satisfied. In the light of the imagery of Pr. 30:16; Is. 5:14; Hab. 2:5 this is possible, but I prefer the view above. *Cf.* 'Two Hebrew Notes', *ASTI*, 5, 1966–7, pp. 82–86.

alone' does not meet our deepest needs.

8. Expositors differ widely on this verse. Most take the first question as purely rhetorical; some (Aalders, following Levy and Thilo) take it as a real question. The second half may then be a further question, or a reply to the first question: 'That which the poor man who knows how to conduct himself also has.'[1] Others see a different question: 'What advantage does the poor man have over him who knows how to…?'[2] Or: 'Why should a poor man know how to face life?'[3]

The Preacher seems to ask two questions, implying a negative answer: Does the wise man have an advantage in this life? Does it help the poor man that he learns to ingratiate himself before others and so improve his lot? The last word may mean 'life' or 'the living'. The mention of *the poor man* indicates the continuance of the themes of poverty and wealth. To *walk before* someone is to live so as to please him (*cf.* 1 Ki. 2:4).

9. The Preacher explains further. If the wise man and the poor man who seeks improvement have *wandering desire*, they are no better off. The *eyes* are one part of man's physical equipment with which to enjoy life and find contentment (*cf.* 1:8 contrasting with 11:9). But though there may be plenty to see, an inward *wandering desire* prevents man from ever being entirely content.

vii. An impasse (6:10–12). **10.** To 'give something a name' is to study or (as here) to appoint its character.[4] Both the world *(what is)* and *man* have settled characters. *One who is stronger than he* is God. Thus the Preacher is underlining the impossibility of changing the basic character of life. Man cannot escape his limitations, nor can he completely unravel the world's anomalies (*cf.* 1:15). He may, like Job, wish to debate the matter with God, but God is altogether greater.

11. Words cannot change the world; they may even add to its futility.

12. Previously the Preacher had asked who appreciates the nature of man's life as it goes beyond death (3:21, Heb.); now he asks who is able to point out what will truly satisfy as a basis of

---

[1] Aalders, understanding *mah* as a relative pronoun (*cf.* Nu. 23:3; Jdg. 9:28).

[2] Wright, understanding *min* as a double duty preposition. Others (*e.g.* Hertzberg) emend the text with the same result.

[3] Gordis, citing the construction in Jb. 1:6.

[4] John Gray (*The Legacy of Canaan* (1965), p. 285) cites a passage in a Ras Shamra text in which to 'declare a name' has a similar meaning. It is less clear that 'its destiny is known' (reading *wᵉnôḏāʿ ʾašrēhû*) is a necessary parallel.

life. What is needed is something which will be adequate for every day (*according to the number of the days*), which will be lifelong and not merely passing (*in life*), which can cope with the inherent futility of the earthly realm (*his vain life*), and the brevity of man (compared to a *shadow*, as in 8:13). *Who knows...?* is followed by *Who can tell man...?* (*cf.* 3:21f.). The two types of question indicate a double problem. The generality of men have no wisdom in themselves (*Who knows...?*); nor can others easily be found to help (*Who can tell...?*). As Kidner puts it: 'He is left with no absolute values to live for ("what is good?"); not even any practical certainties ("what will be?") to plan for.'[1] Like the Mosaic law (*cf.* Gal. 3:22), the Preacher is slamming every door except the door of faith.

C. SUFFERING AND SIN (7:1 – 8:1)

The proverbial units of this section deal with aspects of life that anger or infuriate. The early proverbs deal with death or suffering (7:1–4, 7, 10, 14). Seven proverbs in 7:1–3, 5, 8, 10) are comparisons involving the words 'better than', a common proverbial style. Since the Preacher was a collector of proverbs (12:9f.), these may be a fragmentary collection of 'Better than' proverbs, though the subject-matter provides a fundamental unity.

First the reader is shown the possible instructiveness of sufferings (1–6), then the dangers of trials, compromise, impatience, anger, discontent (7–10). Wisdom is indispensable (11f.); life is under the hand of God (13f.). Thus the first half of ch. 7 follows up the theme of Ecclesiastes as a whole with the question: Will the life of faith survive hard and troublesome times when the 'good old days' have gone and the 'days of adversity' come? The second half of the chapter moves from the crookedness of life (13) to that of mankind (29). Basic questions touching the origin, universality, inequity and perverseness of evil are posed in a mixture of factual statement and exhortation, urging also the need for wisdom which is so rare and remote (19, 23f.) and concluding in 8:1 with a further appeal for wisdom.

i. Instruction from sufferings (7:1–6). 1. There is no need to hold that the first half of v.1 is 'a proverbial phrase which has

[1] Kidner, p. 62.

no relation to the context' (Barton), or a conventional proverb followed by an unconventional deduction (Gordis). We may translate: '*As* a name is better than oil, *so* the day of death is better than the day of birth', thus avoiding the anomaly of a dangling irrelevance. The first half may well have been a popular saying; if so, the Preacher is comparing his point (1b) with a well-known distinction (1a; *cf.* Song 1:3). Hebrew comparisons often put two statements alongside each other leaving out 'As... so' (*cf.* Pr. 17:3). The word-play of *name* (*šēm*) and *oil* (*šemen*) is preserved in Williams' 'Better is name than nard' and Martin's 'Fair fame is better than fine perfume'.[1]

In Israel a *name* was no mere label but intended to express an underlying nature. What is in view is not simply *a good name* (which may be undeserved), but a reputation which flows from character. Such a name was highly valued; even God at the time of the exodus 'got himself a name' (Ne. 9:10).[2]

As inner character is more crucial than outer fragrance, so it is the funeral, not the rowdy birthday party, that poses the ultimate questions about life the Preacher is pressing. This severe statement arises not from despondency but from sheer realism.

2. A further surprise comes and the explanation follows: *the living lay it to heart.* Death brings us to think about life (*cf.* Ps. 90:12), especially since mourning was taken very seriously (*cf.* Gn. 50:10). A party has no such effect. Every funeral anticipates our own.

3. That *the heart* '...may be put right' or '...is put right' is the appropriate translation (better than *made glad*), for it means that the inner life may be 'better situated' for making right judgments and estimations, 'put right' in one's approach to life (*cf.* NIV). A man who has looked death in the face may have his inner life transformed for the better, – not, however, that there is any automatic effect of suffering.

4. The *heart* (NEB *thoughts*) is amongst other things the centre of a man's attention (Ex. 7:23), thought (Dt. 7:17), understanding (1 Ki. 3:9) and memory (Dt. 4:9). One's *heart* being in *the house of mourning* means that death is the object of the wise man's reflections; he allows it to rouse him to thought and concern. The *fool* (*kᵉsîl*), on the other hand, is blind to spiritual issues

[1] G. C. Martin, *Proverbs, Ecclesiastes, and Song of Songs* (1908), p. 253.
[2] See further art. 'Name', *IBD*, pp. 1050–1053; J. A. Motyer, *The Revelation of the Divine Name* (1959).

(Ec. 2:14), yet content in his blindness (Pr. 1:22), verbose yet empty-headed (Pr. 18:2), a menace to society (Pr. 14:7). Not surprisingly his preoccupation is with *the house of feasting*, presumably a place where men indulge in festivity, perhaps a rowdy party.

5. It has been maintained that *the song of fools* means 'the song of praise and flattery', 'the compliments showed by fools' (*cf.* GNB, NEB). But since the word *song* (*šîr*) is always used of quite literal songs (more than seventy times in the Old Testament), it is more likely that the reference is to the songs of jubilation in the house of festivity.[1] The *rebuke of the wise* is exemplified in 2 Samuel 12:1–12; the song of the fool in Amos 6:5f.

6. The pun 'Like the sound of *sîrîm* (thorns) under the *sîr* (pot, cauldron)' is caught by Moffatt's *Like nettles crackling under kettles*. Thorns were a rapidly burning, easily extinguishable fuel in the ancient world (Ps. 58:9). Thus fools' laughter is a sudden flame, a fine display of sparks, accompanied by plenty of noise, but soon spent and easily put out. The last phrase notes that the superficiality of the *fool* is part of life's *vanity*, which elsewhere is said to characterize both the environment of man (1:22ff.) and man himself (6:12).

ii. Four dangers (7:7–10). 7. The opening word in the Hebrew (*kî*) has been taken as an explanation ('For...', *cf.* Leupold), but this does not seem to explain v.6, whose concluding phrase appears to end a paragraph. More probably the word introduces a strong assertion, *Surely...* (as in most translations).[2] Thus vv.7–10 introduce the less beneficial effects of trials. Oppression 'makes a man mad' and may cause even a wise man to lose his head (*cf.* Dt. 28:33f.). Similarly the whole inner life of man may be brought to spiritual ruin by the temptations that belong to an oppressive regime.

To secure a perfect parallelism some have understood *oppression*

[1] This statement is reversed in Jones, but no evidence is cited. Old Testament usage seems to support the statement above.

[2] Because of the slight difficulty the *kî* has been regarded as a textual slip (for it seems to have no equivalent in ancient translations). Others (*e.g.* Lauha) think some words have fallen out between vv. 6 and 7. Others think that the last phrase of v.6 belongs to v.7 ('and even this is vanity, for...'). Hertzberg thinks vv.11 and 12 should be between vv.6 and 7. Yet others regard the whole verses as a gloss. None of these expedients is necessary; an emphatic *kî* is well attested. (*Cf.* R. Gordis, 'The Asseverative Kaph in Ugaritic and Hebrew', *JAOS*, 63, 1943, pp. 176–178.) The RSV translates *kî* as asseverative in, *e.g.*, Jb. 5:2; 28:1; Pr. 30:2; Am. 3:7 as well as in Ec. 7:7.

(NIV *extortion*) to refer to the exercise of it rather than the suffering under it (JB *laughter...merriment* follows an amended text). The Preacher would thus be urging that the 'very exercise of oppression tends to infatuate and bewilder' (Wardlaw; so too Aalders). Alternatively the Hebrew word (*'ōšeq*) has been taken to mean 'bribe' (Gordis, following M. Seidel) or 'slander' (the ancient versions, understanding it as an Aramaism; they are followed by G. R. Driver);[1] this secures a synonymous parallelism. Verses 1–14, however, deal with the suffering of oppression, not its exercise. It is better, therefore, to see here not synonymous parallelism (expressing the same thought) but synthetic parallelism (taking the thought further). The first line, then, speaks of a pressure which oppression may exert on the faithful; the second goes further and provides an example of how a wise man may be 'made mad' by another kind of folly. AV *gift* is literal; NIV, RSV *bribe* catches the sense.

8. The second warning concerns patience. NAB *end of speech* takes a Hebrew word (*dābār*) in its other meaning, but *end of a thing* fits better and has the assent of most translators. In a number of passages *end* has the sense of 'outcome', 'end-product'[2] (*cf.* Pr. 14:12) and this is suitable here. The proverb implies that times of trial may be purposeful, that they are confined to limited seasons, that the end-product makes them worth while (*cf.* Jas. 1:2–4). Thus the reader is invited to grasp the hope of an 'outcome' to trials and to face them accordingly. This will enable him to overcome premature complaint, boasting or arrogance and thus be *patient in spirit*. The antithesis *patient... proud* suggests that patience is an aspect of humility and impatience a proud irritation at God's ways with men (Pr. 16:5).

9. *Anger* (Heb. *ka'as*) is anger tinged with exasperation and elsewhere indicates 'indignation' over idolatry (1 Ki. 15:30) or unmerited treatment (1 Sa. 1:6, 16), 'exasperation' over an erring child (Pr. 17:25) and 'resentment' of a nagging wife (Pr. 27:3). In Ecclesiastes it expresses the exasperation at the perplexities of life (1:18; 2:23), the bitter grief of bereavement (7:3), and here the resentment roused by unjust persecution. It is

---

[1] *VT*, 4, 1954, p. 229. Driver also suggest *mattānāh* be amended to *m'ṭānāh* or *moṭnōh* and translates 'and it (a false accusation) destroys his stout heart'. The combination of a hypothetical word and a speculative reading makes this at best doubtful.

[2] *Cf.* study of *aḥᵃrîṭ* in G. Vos, *The Pauline Eschatology* (1953), pp. 1–7.

stronger than Dahood's 'care'[1] or NAB *discontent*. If tolerated, resentment makes its permanent home in the personality of the fool (*cf.* Heb. 12:15), for *bosom* (AV, RSV) indicates the innermost part of something (1 Ki. 22:35).

10. Each age has its particular difficulties and opportunities. 'The night will come when no man can work,' said Jesus (Jn. 9:4), but the Preacher holds that it is no part of wisdom to herald its arrival prematurely. Wright illustrates the point from the gloom of the older generation at the building of the second temple (Ezr. 3:12–13); the day of small things (Zc. 4:10) was in fact a step towards the coming of Christ. Ginsburg points to the Israelites' longing for Egypt (Ex. 16:3; Nu. 11:5–6; 14:1–4). To evaluate the times may be needful; to ask specifically for days gone by is wrong and foolish. One cannot face the difficulties of one age by pining for another.

iii. The need of wisdom (7:11–12).

11. The previous verses again highlight the need of *wisdom*. The *inheritance* was the land belonging supremely to the LORD but allocated among his people (Ex. 15:17; Nu. 26:53). It could not pass out of the tribe or the family (Nu. 27:8–11; 36:7–9).[2] The Hebrew could be translated 'Wisdom is good *with* an inheritance' or '...as good as an inheritance' (Heb. *'im* meaning 'in common with', 'like', 'as...as' is found in Ps. 73:5b; Ec. 2:16 and elsewhere). In the first case the thought is that family wealth is desirable – the Bible never sees any inherent blessing in poverty – but unaccompanied by wisdom it will not sustain in times of adversity. If 'as...as' is the right translation, wisdom is being compared to an inheritance: it comes supremely from the LORD (*cf.* Dt. 4:21), is greatly to be desired (*cf.* Pr. 3:13–18), and should be the inalienable possession of the people of God.

12. This should be translated: 'To be in the shadow of wisdom is like being in the shadow of[3] silver; and knowledge is

---

[1] M. Dahood, 'Hebrew-Ugaritic Lexicography III', *Bib*, 46, 1965, p. 330.

[2] See further art. 'Inheritance', *IBD*, pp. 691f.

[3] In the MT the two *beth*'s are used in much the same way as two *kaph*'s would be used in a comparison (*cf.* Gn. 18:25; Ho. 4:9). Some scholars wish to emend the text to *kᵉṣēl...kᵉṣēl* (as was read apparently by most ancient translations) or to *bᵉṣēl...kᵉṣēl*. Others (*e.g.* Aalders, Gordis) defend the MT and think the usage is akin to the *beth essentiae*. The present writer is inclined to read *bᵉṣēl...kᵉṣēl;* but if MT is correct, the second *bᵉṣēl* is still to be translated 'like being in the shadow of'. Dahood wishes to drop the second *beth* altogether (CPIQ, p. 209).

an advantage; wisdom keeps the life[1] of him who has it.' To be 'in the shadow of silver'[2] refers to the protective power of wealth. Like riches, knowledge and wisdom protect, but at a deeper level. If J. Gray[3] is right in believing that the Hebrew (*ṣēl*) may mean (i) protection or (ii) glitter (*cf.* Ugaritic *ẓl ksp*, 'glitter of silver'), there is a play on words here.

iv. Life under the hand of God (7:13–14).

13. This echoes 1:15; the crookedness of the world, which is being expounded throughout, is not mere 'fate'. It is subject to God's will (*cf.* Rom. 8:20). We may wish to quarrel with it, but we can effect no change in the basic structure of things.

14. Both *prosperity* and *adversity* have their uses. One leads to joy, the other draws attention to the realities of life and leads (if so allowed) to a life of faith in a sovereign God. Both are subject to God's will and part of his providence. The constant fluctuation between them keeps us dependent not on our own guess-work, but on God who 'holds the key to all unknown'.[4]

v. Dangers along the way (7:15–18).

15. *My vain life* is that dominated by the problems expounded in 1:2–11. The introduction of a vertical perspective does not nullify the overall problem: life remains subject to vanity. The Preacher aims neither to abolish nor even to explain life's anomalies, but to enable one to live with them. It is a simple fact that the *righteous* may, like Naboth (1 Ki. 21:13), *perish in his righteousness*, whereas the wickedness of a Jezebel (1 Ki. 18 – 19; 21) may persist. The anomaly frequently perplexed the devout Israelite (*cf.* Jb.; Pss. 37; 73; Hab. 1:13–17). The blunt statement with no explanation (except perhaps 7:29) demands simply that the believer face life in this world as it really is. Forewarned is forearmed (*cf.* 1 Pet. 4:12).

16. The Preacher warns against two opposing moral dangers.

---

[1] W. Crosser ('The Meaning of "Life" (Ḥayyim) in Proverbs, Job and Ecclesiastes', *Transactions of Glasgow University Oriental Society*, 15, 1953–4, pp. 48–53) points out that 'life' in the Old Testament often refers to more than 'the trivial round and common task' and indicates a satisfying and God-orientated life (*cf.* Pr. 2:19; 10:11, *etc.*). He translates 'shall have life indeed'.

[2] For the bearing of this phrase upon translation hypotheses, *cf.* CPIQ, p. 209.

[3] J. Gray, *The Legacy of Canaan* (1965), p. 285.

[4] NAB *so that man cannot find fault with him* (God) *in anything* is an unlikely translation.

The first some interpreters take as indifference to morality (*cf.* Barton) or a pagan 'moderation in all things'. Others feel that the emphasis is on legalistic righteousness and means 'Do not strive too hard in legalistic observances'. R. N. Whybray on the other hand argues persuasively that what is discouraged is not excessive righteousness but self-righteousness.[1] The Preacher holds that there is no righteous man (7:20). 'Do not be greatly righteous' must be taken ironically and must refer to the way a person thinks about himself and presents himself. The translation *too* or *overmuch* goes somewhat beyond the Hebrew, which means 'greatly' and does not express the judgment implicit in 'too great' or 'overmuch'. This view is confirmed in the next line where the Hebrew for *Do not make yourself overwise* (RSV) contains a Hebrew hithpael which may mean 'to play the wise man' (*cf.* Nu. 16:13 'play the part of a prince'; and 2 Sa. 13:5 'pretend to be ill'). Play-acting righteousness delights in the reputation of wisdom (*cf.* Mt. 23:7).

17. The contrary danger is capitulation to evil. *Greatly* (RSV *overmuch*) does not imply that wickedness in moderation is acceptable! To have omitted *overmuch*, apart from breaking the parallel with v.16, would have contradicted vv.20, 29. The Preacher recognizes wickedness as a fact of human experience. The right life walks the path between two extremes, shunning self-righteousness, but not allowing one's native wickedness to run its own course. The end-product of wickedness run riot may be an untimely death (Ps. 55:23).

18. *The one...the other* refers back to the two dangers of which vv.16f. warned. The righteous person must see both clearly and walk between them, motivated by reverence towards God: it is *he who fears God* that *shall come forth from them all*. The Hebrew *all* is sometimes used when only two items are in view; it should then be translated 'both'.[2] This awe-inspired regard for God is the beginning of knowledge and wisdom (Pr. 1:7; 9:10) and serves as one of the many links between Old and New Covenants (*cf.* Rev. 15:4).

---

[1] Whybray relates this to the form of the verb which is *'al-t^ehî ṣaddîq*, not *'al tiṣdaq*, suggesting that the longer construction combined with the hithpael of the next line points to an interpretation along the line of that suggested above. *Cf.* 'Qoheleth the Immoralist? Qoh. 7:16–17', *Israelite Wisdom: Samuel Terrien Festschrift* (ed. J. G. Gammie *et al.*, 1978), pp. 191–204.

[2] In later Hebrew 'to come forth' may mean 'to do one's duty'; thus Gordis translates 'he who reverences God will do his duty by both'. But it is better to take the verb as meaning 'escape', as in 1 Sa. 14:41.

vi. The need of wisdom (7:19–22). **19.** Both general attitude (*fear*) and detailed application (*wisdom*) are required if the right path between moral legalism and moral indifference is to be maintained. It is difficult to decide whether *ten rulers in a city* uses ten as an indefinite number (Jones; *cf.* Gn. 31:7) or refers to the number of a city council (Gordis, citing Josephus' *Antiquities* xx.8.11; *Vita* 13 and 57). Either way, the meaning is that wisdom in the fear of God may be greater than the collective wisdom of a group of experienced leaders. Power from within is needed, more than advice from without.

20. The argument of vv. 16–19 is brought to a climax, echoing Solomon's words in 1 Kings 8:46. It is put emphatically (with the Heb. emphatic *kî, surely*); it is a universal truth (*not a righteous man on earth*); it covers sins of omission (*does good*) and commission (*never sins*).

21. Human sinfulness is seen particularly in unreliability of speech (*cf.* Jas. 3:2). The corollary is that we are not to pay unnecessary attention to the vindictiveness of others (*cf.* 1 Sa. 24:9), for it will unsettle our tranquillity.

22. Our own experience is sufficient proof that vindictiveness arises from human sinfulness and is frequently inaccurate.

vii. The inaccessibility of wisdom (7:23–24). **23.** Having explored the problems of life by his God-given (2:26) wisdom, the Preacher has realized that wisdom cannot answer the ultimate questions (*cf.* 1:17f.), particularly death (2:15f.). It is this 'ultimate' wisdom, the Preacher says, that was *far from me*.

24. The argument of Ecclesiastes demands that we refer *That which is* not only to all that exists (Gordis' 'all that is come into being'), but also to the very way in which it is constituted by God. It is all that exists as God controls and decrees it that is beyond the Preacher's comprehension. God appoints man's life and environment (*cf.* 1:13; 3:10f., *etc.*). As Moffatt puts it: *Reality is beyond my grasp*, says the Preacher. *Who can find...?* is a rhetorical question. No-one can grasp God's plan and purpose.

viii. The sinfulness of man (7:25–29). **25.** The Preacher's realization of the limits of his wisdom drives him to ponder further the character of man. RSV *the sum of things* derives from a word meaning 'to reckon' in both the mathematical and intellectual sense, and translates it as 'thought' in 9:10. Here the point is that the Preacher has pondered long and hard the enigmas of human character. What did it all amount to? The welter of intellectual and moral terms, *know...search...seek, wisdom...reason, wickedness...folly...foolishness...madness,* again emphasizes his point and indicates his thoroughness.

26. The Preacher sets out his conclusions; first, about a particular kind of woman. She is *more bitter than death,* her personality (*heart*) is dominated by the instincts of the hunter (*snares and nets*), and she is forceful in her attentions (*hands* as *prison fetters*). The wisdom to perceive the snares and traps is given only to one *who pleases God* (*cf.* 2:26). Any accusation of misogyny misses the Preacher's point, as we see from the contrasting picture of married love in 9:9.

27–28. The Preacher then sets out his conclusions about men and women in general. Mathematical imagery still pervades this section. The Preacher wants to know what the sinfulness of man adds up to. The passage is still dealing with wisdom (*cf.* vv.23, 25); this is in his mind when he draws a distinction between the sexes. Wisdom, he says, is rare in men, but rarer in women. Such a statement is not unique to Ecclesiastes (*cf.* 2 Tim. 3:6); he need not be thought a bachelor (Gordis) or one disappointed in love (Plumptre). The statement is historical, unlike the generalized statement of v.29. Emphasis is not on what the Preacher found, but on what he found lacking. In either sex wisdom is rare; 'he finds men only one-tenth of one percent better than women!' (Gordis). Ancient Near Eastern literature contains more extreme statements (*e.g.* 'Woman is an iron dagger – a sharp one, which cuts a man's neck')[1] which find no parallel in Ecclesiastes.

29. This verse presents the Preacher's conclusions about the whole human race. The first Hebrew word (*l'ḇaḏ*) means 'above' or 'by itself',[2] and the opening words may be literally translated 'on its own (*l'ḇaḏ*), see, this I found...'. The Preacher is driven to a single point which is the source of the calamities previously described (vv.15–28): here is the grand total of his spiritual calculations. The blame for the rarity of wisdom is attributed to no-one but mankind himself. He was created neither sinful, nor neutral, but *upright,* a word used of the state of the heart which is disposed to faithfulness or obedience (*cf.* 2 Ki. 10:15, Heb.; Ps. 7:11).[3] Despite an original uprightness, sin has

---

[1] *ANET,* p. 425.   [2] *Cf.* BDB, p. 94.

[3] *Cf.* D. J. Wiseman, 'Law and Order in Old Testament Times', *Vox Evangelica,* 8, 1973, pp. 5–21, esp. pp. 5f.

'entered in' (*cf.* Gn. 3:1–7; Rom. 5:12). Man's sin is perverse (AV *invention* means a deliberate contrivance for overcoming what would otherwise be expected), deliberate (*sought* indicates something positive and persistent), universal (*they* individualizes *man* mentioned earlier; *cf.* 1 Ki. 8:46; Rom. 3:23), multiform (*many* points to the variety of manifestations of sin: 'every one to his own way', Is. 53:6). Kidner points to the contrast with a passage in the *Babylonian Theodicy* where the gods are blamed for man's wickedness: 'With lies, and not truth, they endowed them for ever.'[1] *Behold* draws attention to the fact and assures us it is there for all to see. *This I found* shows that the Preacher's theology was confirmed by life itself.

ix. Who is really wise? (8:1). This verse belongs more to what precedes than to what follows, for it forms a fitting conclusion to proverbs which have appealed for wisdom in relation to suffering and sin; it is reminiscent of a similar final challenge at the end of Hosea (14:9). The Hebrew word translated *like* sometimes speaks of exact likeness to an ideal. It could be translated 'Who is really wise…?'. *Interpretation* (*pēser*) is the word well-known to students of the Qumran scrolls, where it is used of the distinctive out-of-context interpretations of the Old Testament by the Qumran community. Another form of the word (*pitrôn*) is used in Genesis of the interpretation of dreams (Gn. 40:5). Where, asks the Preacher, is the man who discerns his way through the problems detailed in 7:1–29, and who will interpret aright the mysteries of providence? The shining *face* generally speaks of favour (*cf.* Nu. 6:25). Here it speaks of the wise man who is visibly gracious in his demeanour, and (as the next phrase says) whose gentleness is obvious in his facial expression (contrast Dt. 28:50; Dn. 8:23).[2]

D. AUTHORITY, INJUSTICE AND THE LIFE OF FAITH (8:2–9:10)

The justification for treating this as a single section in the Preacher's mind is that the sequence of thought runs parallel to

---

[1] Kidner, p. 73; *cf.* Lambert, p. 89.
[2] Gordis and others who take the verse with Ec. 8:2ff. understand it to refer to discretion at court. NEB follows an emended text to give …*make a man hated* (*cf.* also NAB).

1:2 – 3:22 (see p. 55). He faces the grim realities of kingly authority (8:2–9) and the injustices of life (8:10–15), and perplexed with the enigma of life (8:16–17) and the ultimate certainty of death (9:1–6), he again turns to a position of faith as the only remedy (9:7–10).

i. Royal authority (8:2–8). After a note of command in vv.2–4, the theme gradually widens into more general proverbs dealing with authority (5–8).

2–3a. The first few words of the Hebrew are enigmatic (reading literally 'I – attend to[1] the mouth of the king') but may be paraphrased 'I advise you, be attentive to what the king says'. The seemingly unattached 'I' has perplexed translators. Most assume that a verb such as 'say' or 'counsel' is understood (AV, RV). Others ignore the word entirely (LXX, Peshitta, Targum, RSV), amend it to 'My son' (Wildeboer), or the sign of the accusative (Barton, Scott), or assume that 'say' has dropped out of the text (Wright). The enigma is as yet unsolved, but the general sense is clear. The *mouth of the king*[2] is not simply his commands (as in most translations), but more generally 'what he says' (*cf.* Pr. 13:3). The latter part of the verse gives the reason for the command: ... *and that on account of the oath of God* (*cf.* AV, RV; RSV receives comment below). Evidently it was a custom for the king's subjects to take an oath of loyalty. 2 Chronicles 36:13 and Ezekiel 17:13 have been cited as throwing some light on the matter, but here the oath is one taken more generally among the populace (*cf.* 1 Ch. 29:24; Josephus, *Antiquities* xv.10.4; xvii.2.4). A less likely view, that of Hertzberg, takes the oath as given by God to the king. Phrases elsewhere parallel to 'oath of God' (Ex. 22:10f.; 2 Sa. 21:7; 1 Ki. 2:42f.) make it more likely that it is an oath taken by men, but sanctioned or approved by God.

A good translation of the first clause of v.3 is NASV *Do not be in a hurry to leave him.* 'To go from someone's presence' elsewhere signifies disaffection or disloyalty (*cf.* Ho. 11:2). Thus the Preacher warns against a capricious desertion of one's post (*cf.*

---

[1] Hebrew *šāmar* may mean 'be careful about' (Pr. 21:23; Mi. 7:5) or 'attend to' (Dt. 28:1; Ps. 119:67 and elsewhere).

[2] Leupold holds that God the heavenly 'king' is in view here. But in other passages where 'king' is used of God (Pss. 5:2; 10:16; 20:9; Is. 6:5), the context makes it clear. Here the *king* seems to be distinct from *God* mentioned in the next phrase.

10:4) and against persistence in any disloyalty (RV *persist* is better than NASV *join in* or RSV *delay*).[1] It is possible, however, to punctuate otherwise and construe the grammar differently. The Hebrew verb *bāhal* may mean 'hasten' or 'fear'. If the latter be adopted, and if the opening phrase belongs to v.2, we have: ...*because of your oath be not dismayed; go from his presence*... (RSV; *cf.* NEB, GNB). In this case v.3 warns against high office. But the parallel in 10:4 argues decisively against RSV and in favour of RV, NASV and similar translations.

3b. In addition to the religious reason of the oath there are more mundane inducements to submission. The Preacher is not above using both methods of appeal (like Paul in Rom. 13:1–7). The king's wishes (*whatever he pleases*) and words are too powerful to disregard.

4. The extent of royal power, including taxation and conscription to royal duties, was underlined in 1 Samuel 8:10–18, which deals with the beginning of the institution and has similarities to records of other contemporary kingdoms.[2]

5. Previously it has been urged that life is to be lived under God's sovereign disposal of events (3:1–15). The same idea is now applied to the difficulties of living under an autocratic king. Submission is not to be blind passivity. RSV *way* (Heb. *mišpāṭ*) means 'custom, procedure' as well as 'verdict, judgment'; the wise man will be alert to God's timing and 'proper procedures', as were Jonathan (1 Sa. 19:4–6), Nathan (2 Sa. 12:1–14) and Esther (Est. 7:2–4).

6. Looking for 'times' and 'procedures' is a general principle for *every matter*. The explanatory phrase, *for the calamity of man is great upon him*, has been taken to refer to (i) a burdensome punishment which rests upon man; (ii) man's inherent weakness or evil: 'A wise courtier will find an opportunity to execute his designs, because human weakness is widespread, and an opening is sure to appear' (Gordis); (iii) Jones's explanation, that 'Man has enough trouble already without asking for further difficulty through open defiance of the king. He should wait and his time

---

[1] The Hebrew *'al-tibbāhēl...tēlēk* is an example of two verbs giving a single idea, one of them with adverbial force. It is similar to Gn. 24:18, 'She hastened and put down', *i.e.* 'she hastily put down'. *Cf.* Barton, Gordis, DS 83(c) and GK 120(g). N. M. Weldman cites Akkadian parallels to this verse in 'The Dābār Ra' of Eccl. 8:3', *JBL*, 98, 1979, pp. 407f.

[2] *Cf.* I. Mendelsohn, *BASOR*, 143, 1956, pp. 17–22; K. A. Kitchen, *Ancient Orient and Old Testament* (1966), pp. 158f.

will come'. Taken within the total context of Ecclesiastes the 'calamity' must be human frustration, perplexity and strain at the oppressive ('great upon man') burden of life. Hence (RSV *although* is better translated 'Because' or 'For', as in RV) the need to mark well the 'times' and 'procedures' of wise action.

7. The key to human perplexity is frustration and ignorance concerning the future. In this we can find help neither in ourselves nor from anyone else.

8. Four limitations to all authority are set forth. First, 'no man is master over the spirit,[1] to confine the spirit'. Some have understood the clause to be identical in meaning to the next, but since the third and fourth are distinct, the first two are best taken as distinct also. The meaning 'confine' is well established; it is used of 'locking up' cattle and 'confining' a prisoner (1 Sa. 6:10; Je. 32:2f.). The cognate noun (*keleʾ*) means 'prison'. No prison can be found which will hold the spirit, the inner life of man, with its longings, impulses and convictions. Our Lord drew a similar distinction (Mt. 10:28). Second, *there is no master over the day of death*. This puts negatively the positive point (3:2) that death is within God's appointed 'times'. Third, 'there is no release[2] in war'. As *the* indicates (in the Hebrew), *the war* in mind is death (hence AV *that war*). This is one realm where 'every man must advance; and every man must advance alone, to single combat; and every man in succession must fall' (Wardlaw). Fourth, 'wickedness[3] will not deliver its owner'. The deliverance envisaged is that from death. No measure, foul or fair, will rescue from this intrusion. Kingly authority meets its match here.

ii. Life's injustices (8:9–11).

9. It is disputed whether this concludes the previous section or opens the next one. In fact it

---

[1] Wright, NASV and NEB take *rûaḥ* to mean 'wind', but the context and association with death makes 'spirit' more likely. The two are linked in 3:19–21; 12:7.

[2] *Mišlaḥat* has been taken to mean 'escape' (Targum, Levy), 'weapon' (Ehrlich, cited by Gordis), or as an elliptical expression for 'putting forth the hand' (Gordis citing Is. 11:14), or as 'discharge' (BDB), 'furlough' (Barton, Delitzsch; *cf.* Dt. 20:1ff.; Herodotus iv. 84; vii. 38f.; Josephus, *Antiquities* xii.9.3; xiii.2.4). Others amend to *mᵉluḥeṣet* ('amulet') (Galling). In Ps. 78:49 an active sense, 'sending away', is found; but *šālaḥ* may have a permissive force 'release' (Ex. 4:21; 5:2), and thus 'release' or something similar may be the meaning here.

[3] NEB apparently takes 'wickedness' (*rešaʿ*) to mean wealth gained by wrongdoing.

bridges the two, for *all this* generally points backwards. Williams maintains the opposite, but 7:23; 9:1; 11:9 and the *all* of 12:13 contradict him. The first word of v.10, however, implies a close connection with v.9. So in summarizing his observations in 8:2–8 the Preacher also starts a new line of thought. Again we see his careful observation (*I observed*) combined with shrewd evaluation (*applying my mind*), his breadth of view (*All this...all that is done*) and his earthbound horizon (*under the sun*). The Hebrew wording (*...a time when man lords it...*) recalls 3:1–15 with its assurance concerning God's control of all of the seasons of life. 'To his hurt' (Heb.) is not *to his own hurt* (AV) but to the hurt of the one under the abuser of power. Two passages containing the same verb 'lord it' (*šālaṭ*) illustrate the point (Ne. 5:15; Est. 9:1).

10. In the Hebrew this is 'one of the most difficult passages in the book'.[1] The final phrase, *This also is vanity*, requires that the passage be reporting something frustrating or vexatious. The preceding and following verses (9, 11–12a) make it likely that this is pointing out some injustice.[2] Only in vv.12b–13 is any statement of faith introduced. RSV grasps the gist, but the details are debatable. The following comments are based mainly on RSV, with variant interpretations in the footnotes.

The opening phrase (RSV *Then*) is used elsewhere only in Esther 4:16, where it apparently means 'In such circumstances'.[3] Here we may translate: 'And in such a case I saw the wicked buried.'[4] A proper burial was part of honourable treatment in ancient Israel, and its omission was considered a great misfortune (Je. 16:6).[5] Even criminals (Dt. 21:22f.), suicides (2 Sa. 17:23) and enemies of the nation (Jos. 8:29) were generally buried (hence the ferocity of Am. 2:1). The Preacher is troubled by the honour that comes to the wicked.

The Hebrew continues: '...and they came[6] and from the holy

[1] C. W. Reines, 'Koheleth VIII, 10', *JJS*, 5, 1954, pp. 86f. He maintains that *wb'wm* should be read instead of *wb'w*, and takes the verse to assert that 'after their death and burial the evil deeds of the wicked are quickly forgotten and their graves are held in veneration'.

[2] Thus the view that the text speaks of retribution falling upon the ungodly (Leupold and others) is unlikely.

[3] So BDB, p. 486.

[4] NEB and NAB ('approach and enter...') read a verb *q-r-b* (draw near, approach) instead of the verb in the MT, *q-b-r* (bury).

[5] *Cf.* art. 'Burial and Mourning', *IBD*, pp. 211–215.

[6] Aalders thinks 'they came' an ellipsis for 'they departed in peace' (a

place they went.' RSV takes this to mean: they went *in and out of
the holy place* [Jerusalem],[1] *and were praised in the city where they had
done such things*.[2] This involves a minute emendation of
wᵉyištakkᵉhu ('they were forgotten') to *wᵉyištabbᵉhu* ('they were
praised'), which is almost certainly correct. The Hebrew letters
beth and *kaph* are similar; there is support in the ancient versions
and in some Hebrew manuscripts. The verse is dealing with an
injustice (*they were praised*), not a rightful retribution (*they were
forgotten*).[3]

11. An explanation follows of the moral indifference and
complacency that lies behind the unrequited injustices of vv.9f.
People misunderstand delay in judgment. Life, health, shelter,
family, food and clothing remain as normal. 'All continues just
as it was' (2 Pet. 3:4). God's seeming inactivity is attributed to
indifference, impotence or favouritism.

The human problem is traced to the *heart* (obscured by GNB,
NEB); we are corrupt at source. That the heart 'becomes full'
(Heb.) *to do evil* indicates a growing brazenness as nothing
intervenes to check the sinner's progress (*cf.* the wording in Est.
7:5, 'Who... is emboldened to do this?'). *Sentence* (*pitgam*,
probably a Persian word) is used elsewhere of royal decrees
(Ezr. 4:19; Est. 1:20) but here refers to divine judgment.

iii. The answer of faith (8:12–13). **12.** The Preacher is
content to wait patiently. The sinner's evil may be great (*a
hundred times*, omitted by NEB) and his life prolonged (*lengthen his
life*), but he holds it as a matter of faith that the vindication of
the righteous is only a question of time. The way of safety is to
fear God. In the wisdom tradition the 'fear' of God is the awe and

---

shorthand expression, the longer form of which occurs in Gn. 15:15 and Is.
57:2. ASV takes it as elliptical for 'they came to the grave', and Wright understands it as 'they came into being'.

[1] Some (*e.g.* Reines, GNB) consider 'the holy place' to be a cemetery. The
usage is unattested. Others take it to be the temple (*cf.* JB *people came from the
temple to honour them*).

[2] The Hebrew for *such things* (*ken*) occasionally is a noun meaning 'right' (*cf.*
Heb. of Nu. 27:7; Je. 8:6). The last phrase may, therefore, mean 'Those who
acted right...' (*cf.* Heb. of 2 Ki. 7:9) and be the subject of the verb. There are
several suggested translations along these lines. Those who translate thus see
two groups in the text, the honourably buried wicked and the forgotten righteous.
Another approach is the Geneva Bible's *where they had done right* (cited by
Ginsburg).

[3] The emendation is accepted by RSV, JB, NAB, GNB, NIV. The NEB adopts the
same reading but takes it reflexively (*they prided themselves*).

holy caution that arises from realization of the greatness of God: 'Splendour...terrible majesty...power...justice...righteousness...Therefore men fear him' (Jb. 37:22–24); when Job throws caution to the winds he is 'doing away with the fear of God' (Jb. 15:4). Though the Preacher is aware of its limitations, he too calls for the 'fear of God'. It is part of his summary of the requirements of wisdom (12:13). The 'seasons' of life need it (3:14); worship demands it (5:1–7). It will bring deliverance (7:18) and ultimate vindication, as is promised here. The repetitive wording, ...*that fear God, that fear before him*, emphasizes its importance. *Before him* points to its chief characteristic, awe in the presence of God's greatness.[1] It is noteworthy that, whereas the Preacher so often says 'I have seen...I saw' (8:9f.), here his reply is introduced by *I know*. The injustices of life are open for all to see; the Preacher's reply is not an observation, but the answer of faith.

13. Equally he is certain that, despite the delay, calamity will finally befall the sinner. Though he may 'lengthen (his days)' (v.12, Heb.), the judgment falling upon him is that he will not *lengthen his days*! The paradox has been elucidated in various ways. Some see a quotation (Gordis; GNB) or the hand of a redactor[2] (*e.g.* Lauha). Leupold sees a play on words which may be paraphrased: 'though he go on long (in sin) he shall not make his days long.' This is possible, since 'his days' occurs in the Hebrew of v.13 but not of v.12. The present writer believes that the Preacher 'drops the veil of secularism' (Kidner) and puts the two statements side by side to be deliberately provocative. It is typical of the duality which pervades Ecclesiastes: from the 'under the sun' viewpoint the sinner is infuriating in his long survival; from the perspective of faith time looks different and the Preacher cannot imagine sin endlessly unrebuked and unjudged (*cf.* Jas. 4:13f.). The paradox also raises the possibility of a life after death, where the sinner will no longer go on in his sin. This is confirmed in that *a shadow* is a figure of the insecurity of human life (*cf.* Pss. 102:11; 109:23). In the light of this, AV *neither shall he prolong his days which are as a shadow* (*cf.* RV) is preferable to RSV *neither will he prolong his days like a shadow*. This accords with the context, and the verse can only mean that the unrighteous will not flourish beyond the grave (*cf.* Pss. 49; 73; Ec. 3:16–21; 12:14).

[1] See further on 12:13.
[2] See however the comments on p. 41.

iv. The problem restated (8:14). The perplexity is restated in more acute form (*cf.* also 3:16; 4:1; 5:8; 7:7): retribution and reward are totally reversed.

v. The remedy recalled (8:15). The Preacher does not try to unravel the enigma completely. Rather he presents a practical solution, along lines now familiar. Again he is concerned about earthly life (*under the sun*), commends joy (*cf.* 2:26; 3:12; 5:18, 20) and contentment (*to eat and drink*; *cf.* 2:24f.; 3:13; 5:18). This is to be our encouragement amid daily life and activity, a life-long (*through the days of life*) close companion (*go with him* translates Heb. *yilwennû*, 'cleave to him', 'join on to him'). The secret of it all is: it is God-given.

vi. The enigma of life (8:16 – 9:1). 16. The progress of thought from 8:2 leads back to the over-all puzzle of life. The Preacher's quest was thorough, involving careful thought over his experience (*wisdom*) as well as observation (*I applied my mind…to see*). The Hebrew is obscure. After the opening, 'When I gave my heart to…', comes a parenthetical remark ('For neither[1] in the day nor in the night do one's[2] eyes see sleep'[3]). The sense is completed in v.17 ('Then I saw…'). Again the Preacher sees that man's problem gives him restless days and sleepless nights (*cf.* 2:23).

17. His conclusion is that we must be content not to know everything. Neither hard work (*toil*), persistent endeavour (*seeking*), skill or experience (*wisdom*) will unravel the mystery. Wise men may make excessive claims; they too will be baffled.

9:1. This might be translated: 'Now, I have taken all this to heart and explain it that righteous men, wise men, and their deeds are in the care of God. Man does not know whether it will be love or hatred; everything awaits him.' The first word is little more than 'Well now'; it is neither an explanation (AV *For*) nor a contrast (RSV *But*). RSV *in the hand of* is a well-known expression meaning 'at the disposal of' (Gn. 14:20; 16:6, *etc.*), 'under the supervision of' (Gn. 9:2, *etc.*), or 'in the care of' (best here; *cf.* Est. 2:3, 8; Jb. 12:10; Ps. 31:5, *etc.*). If, as is widely thought, the

---

[1] So Lauha, Barton, Aalders and others (*cf.* NIV). This view takes *kî gam* as two distinct words ('For both'). Another view (*cf.* Gordis) takes it to mean 'though'. This is reflected in GNB.

[2] The 'he' in the suffix 'his' refers to man as the victim of toil (*cf.* Barton).

[3] *Cf.* Gordis for a Mishnaic parallel to 'seeing sleep'.

second half refers to God's acceptance or rejection of men, the thought will be that 'it takes more than observation to discover how He is disposed towards us' (Kidner). But the *love* and *hatred* mentioned a few sentences later (v.6) are clearly human. Nor does this view cohere easily with statements elsewhere that the righteous have an assurance of God's approval (*cf.* 2:24; 3:12f.; 5:19f.; 9:7–10). More likely, the point is that the treatment the righteous will receive is unknown; who can tell what the future will bring? Righteousness and wisdom have no built-in guarantees of an easy life. The Hebrew *before them*, meaning 'awaiting them', is a rare usage; but though its reference may be spatial (Gn. 32:21, *etc.*), there is no reason why it should not also be temporal.

Following the guidance of ancient versions, RSV takes the first word of MT v.2 (*hkl*, 'everything') as *hbl* ('vanity') and thus translates *Everything before them is vanity*. This is plausible, but MT makes sense as it stands.

vii. 'The sting of death' (9:2–3). 2. The opening phrase is best translated as in RV: *All things come alike to all*. It need not refer exclusively to death, although the passage goes on to that. The point is simply that the righteous are not visibly favoured by providence, nor the unrighteous visibly rebuked by providence. Death itself comes indiscriminately to all. After *to the good* RSV adds *and the evil*, following the guidance of the ancient versions; the additional phrase is not in MT.[1] It is likely that *he who swears* refers not to profane or rash swearing (the majority interpretation; *cf.* Ex. 20:7; Mt. 5:34), but to swearing 'by the LORD's name' (Dt. 6:13; 10:20) which was part of allegiance to the covenant. He who *shuns an oath*[2] (RSV; better than AV *that feareth an oath*, meaning to honour it; *cf.* 1 Sa. 14:26) will refer to one who avoids loyalty to the covenant. This view is upheld by the fact that in the series of contrasts the good characteristic comes first (as Plumptre observes).

3. Death is not a 'natural' phenomenon to the Preacher, but an invincible *evil*. Also linked with *evil* is *madness*, connected elsewhere with glib frivolity (2:2), corruption in society (7:7), folly

---

[1] It may be that a lengthy phrase *for the good, for the clean* balances *and for the unclean*, in order to match the longer phrase (in Heb.) *for the one who does not sacrifice* balancing the short phrase (in Heb.) *the man who offers a sacrifice* (so Gordis, NASV).

[2] *Cf. DTTML*, for *yara'* meaning 'to shun' in late Hebrew.

(10:12f.), self-justifying disobedience (1 Sa. 13:13) and inclinations to violence (1 Sa. 26:21) or pride (2 Sa. 24:10); its usage suggests, therefore, a moral wildness that is impetuous and irrational.[1] The problem of our fallen nature (*cf.* 7:29) is universal, for *evil* is ascribed to the *sons of men* in general. It characterizes the whole inner nature of man (*the heart*), irremediable (life-long, *while they live*), dominant (we are *full of* it). The grimmest aspect (the 'sting', 1 Cor. 15:56) of death is found here, for with such a heart are we brought 'to judgment...to his eternal home...to God' (11:9; 12:5, 7).

viii. Where there's life, there's hope (9:4–6). 4. The first half of the verse does not deny an afterlife (*cf.* 3:21, Heb.; 12:7), but implies that earthly life cannot be enjoyed in retrospect. This is underlined by the proverb in the second half. The *lion*, 'mightiest of the beasts' (Pr. 30:30), was admired in the ancient world. The *dog*, on the other hand, was a despised scavenger (Ex. 22:31; 1 Ki. 14:11), notorious for its uncleanness (Pr. 26:11); a Sumerian proverb states: 'He who esteems highly dogs which are clever is a man who has no shame.'[2] All this adds point to the Preacher's estimation of this life as decisive.

5. The *hope* of v.4 is explained by the opportunity this present life affords to consider the fact of death, as the Preacher has been constantly urging, and to evaluate life accordingly. No description is given of life beyond the grave except the warning of a judgment and the negative point that all earthly experiences cease. Elsewhere *reward* is used of the end-product of human endeavour (4:9), including material goods (Nu. 18:31); death removes us altogether from this realm.

That *the dead know nothing* is not an extreme claim within the Old Testament (*cf.* 2 Ki. 22:20; Jb. 14:21f.). Other cultures in the ancient world had their superstitions concerning contact with the dead, as does ours. Heidel cites a Babylonian text which speaks of 'the terrifying ghost...which pursues me all day [and] terrifies me all night...be it a ghost of my family or of my relationship, be it [the ghost of] a man who died a violent death, [or] be it a wandering ghost'.[3] Among Babylonians and

---

[1] JB assumes that *towards the living* has dropped out of the text. This is unnecessary.
[2] *Cf.* E. I. Gordon, *Sumerian Proverbs* (1959), p. 256; *cf.* other disparaging references to dogs on pp. 256–262. The translation above is provisional.
[3] A. Heidel, *The Gilgamesh Epic and Old Testament Parallels* (1963), p. 157.

Assyrians it was customary for relatives of the departed to supply the graves with food and drink.[1] Such, however, was not the case in Israel. Conversely, the living forget the dead; despite promises and memorials, they are soon 'out of mind' (Ps. 31:12).

6. Among earthly experiences which will cease are *love* and *hate*. The next word often means *zeal* (NASV) or *jealousy* (NIV), but here a more general term, such as GNB *their passions*, suits the context. The phrase *under the sun* confirms that the previous verses have in view the irreparable loss of earthly life. One's *portion* (AV) or *share* (RSV) is the measure of joy and satisfaction that comes through one's daily activities (*cf*. 3:22; 5:18, where it is sometimes translated *lot*), found not in self-centred pleasures (2:1–11) but only when taken as the gift of God (3:22; 5:19). The Preacher repeatedly warns that it cannot be recaptured after death. Here is the strongest statement of the point: at death its passing is total (*no more*) and permanent (*for ever*).

ix. The remedy of faith (9:7–10).

7. A note of imperious exhortation breaks in: *Go...!* What had previously been put as advice (2:24–26; 3:12f., 22; 5:18–20) is now an urgent summons to action. The believer must give himself to a contented life (*cf*. comments on *eat* under 5:18) and to a joyful life (*cf*. also 11:9). The basis of contentment is that *God has already approved what you do*. This almost Pauline touch is the nearest the Preacher came to a doctrine of justification by faith. Man has but to receive contentment as God's gift (*cf*. 3:13); God will approve of him and his works. The believer is not struggling for acceptance; he is 'already' accepted. On that basis (moving from Paul to James, one might say) the wise man 'works with all his might' (9:10).

8. *White garments* and anointing *oil* made life more comfortable in a hot climate, the latter relieving the irritations of dry skin. Food, clothing and ointment are mentioned in a number of ancient texts as necessities of life (*cf*. Ho. 2:5; Lk. 7:38, 46).[2] The Egyptian *Song of the Harper* spoke of 'myrrh upon thy head and

---

[1] *Ibid.*, p. 204. *Cf*. also Miranda Bayliss' references to expiatory rituals for the dead in Assyria and Babylonia ('The Cult of Dead Kin in Assyria and Babylonia', *Iraq*, 35, 1973, pp. 115–125, esp. p. 117).

[2] *Cf*. J. Zandell, 'Egyptological Commentary on the Old Testament', *Travels in the World of the Old Testament* (ed. S. H. G. Heerma Van Voss *et al*., 1974), pp. 279f.

clothing of fine linen'.[1] An even more striking parallel is found in the *Epic of Gilgamesh*:

> Gilgamesh, whither rovest thou?
> The life thou pursuest thou shalt not find.
> When the gods created mankind,
> Death for mankind they set aside,
> Life in their own hands retaining.
> Thou, Gilgamesh, let full be thy belly,
> Make thou merry by day and by night.
> Of each day make thou a feast of rejoicing,
> Day and night dance thou and play!
> Let thy garments be sparkling fresh,
> Thy head be washed; bathe thou in water.
> Pay heed to the little one that holds on to thy hand,
> Let thy spouse delight in thy bosom!
> For this is the task of (mankind)![2]

Ecclesiastes, however, does not advocate hedonism under the shadow of the gods' ill-will, but contentment as part of God's gift, the outflow of an assurance of acceptance by him.

9. Marriage is a further help in the midst of the frustrations of life. It is envisaged as man's normal state, for it is urged upon his readers in general (*cf.* Gn. 2:18). As in Genesis 2, the man is envisaged as bearing the prime responsibility of life, with the woman as his companion, a solace in the midst of a *vain life* (*cf.* 1 Cor. 11:8f.; 1 Tim. 2:13). The demands of marriage include the giving of affection (*whom you love*; *cf.* Eph. 5:25), the active quest for enjoyment (*Enjoy life,* RSV), a life-long (*all...your...life*) encouragement amid the responsibilities and duties of life (*in your toil at which you toil*).

Two considerations reinforce the appeal. First, marriage is God's gift and thus its inherent goodness is assured (*cf.* Heb. 13:4); *portion* is the Preacher's term for the pleasures and solaces which God is pleased to give us in the midst of earthly vanity (see on 3:22, p.89). Second, life is only too brief and insecure (*your vain life*); since marriage is numbered among earthly blessings (*under the sun*), this life is the time for its enjoyment and will soon be lost.[3]

---

[1] See text cited on p. 34.   [2] *ANET*, p. 90.

[3] Because the term for *wife* here is simply 'woman', and because the Heb. lacks the article and could mean 'a woman', it is thought by some (*e.g.* Barton, Ginsburg) that the Preacher is urging sensuality without marriage. This neglects

10. The series of encouragements leads naturally to this one, for contentment (v.7), comfort (v.8) and companionship (v.9) enable a man to throw himself into the tasks of life with energy and confidence.

The *hand* refers to strength or ability (*cf.* Jos. 8:20 AV mg., RV mg.); *finds* speaks of opportunity (*cf.* 1 Sa. 9:8, where 'Here is found' (Heb.) means 'Here I happen to have with me'). To do *whatever your hand finds to do*, therefore, is to give oneself to life with its joys and its responsibilities, according to one's ability and circumstances. Life is to be active and energetic (*with all your might*), practical (*thought* means 'device', 'stratagem', 'idea'), informed (*knowledge*) and skilful (*wisdom*). Such characteristics of the life of faith are possible only during a man's lifetime. The emptiness of the pessimist's life, if it finds no remedy, cannot be filled up in retrospect.

Having come to the end, *Sheol,* the place of dead, earthly experiences – activity, plans, wisdom – cease (*cf.* Jn. 9:4). The Preacher does not provide any positive description of *Sheol.* Negatively it is characterized by the absence of opportunity for earthly life; more than that he does not say. Unlike other nations in antiquity,[1] Israel can scarcely be said to have had a developed mythology of the underworld. *Sheol,* a proper noun of uncertain etymology, is a place-name, but has been demythologized and within the Old Testament is no more than the state of death pictured in visible terms.

E. WISDOM AND FOLLY (9:11 – 10:20)

In the opinion of many commentators there is no sustained argument in these verses. Gordis speaks of the 'variety of subject matter and the lack of logical organization in this section'.

---

the background of Ecclesiastes in Genesis 1–11; also the style of Heb. in Ecclesiastes (whatever may be its date or origin) tends to omit the article where other writers would have it. It is, therefore, precarious to base too much upon its absence (*cf.* R. Gordis, 'The Original Language of Qoheleth', *JQR*, 37, 1946, pp. 81ff.). The companionship envisaged is life-long, not a casual liaison.
[1] *Cf.* N. J. Tromp, *Primitive Conceptions of Death and the Nether World* (1969), ch. 2; P. Watson, *Mot, the God of Death, at Ugarit and in the Old Testament* (University Microfilms, 1971); J. Zandee, *Death as an Enemy According to Ancient Egyptian Conceptions* (1960); E. F. Sutcliffe, *The Old Testament and the Future Life* (1947), chs. 1–2 for extra-biblical ideas.

Delitzsch complained, 'How much time, thought and paper have been wasted in order to connect this verse-group with the preceding!' A few scholars, however, (Leupold, Hertzberg and others) have attempted to trace an argument. Leupold thought 'that the author is writing coherent discourse and has logical sequence of thought' (comment on 10:1). The truth of the matter is not easily determined. Certainly attempts to trace a detailed argument have been unconvincing; on the other hand coherence of argument is different from coherence of subject-matter. If the former is not in evidence in these verses, the latter is to a large extent, for each unit deals directly in some way with folly or wisdom.

i. Time and chance (9:11–12). First, the verses introduce the themes of wisdom and its limits, as well as counterbalancing vv.7–10. The wise man must not be so taken up with the contented life as to forget life's frustrations; for these do not disappear when the wise man is assured of God's approval.

11. Five accomplishments are listed, none of which guarantees success or prosperity: (i) the swift-footed may find himself a loser (*cf.* 2 Sa. 2:18); (ii) military strength is no guarantee of success in battle (*cf.* Is. 36 – 37); (iii) wisdom similarly is no guarantee of a livelihood (*cf.* Ec. 9:13–16; 10:1); (iv) understanding may be accompanied by poverty (*cf.* 9:15); (v) favour may be delayed for innocent Joseph (Gn. 37 – 41) and not come at all for others (Ec. 9:13–16). Two factors may upset all human calculations. First, *time* limits us, an echo of the teaching throughout Ecclesiastes that the seasons of our life are in the hand of God; this is a warrant for faith but also a death-blow for self-confidence. Second, *chance* is the unexpected event which may throw the most accomplished off course, despite the most thoroughly prepared schemes.[1]

12. The seasons of life are unpredictable (*man does not know them* in advance), inescapable (*an evil net…a snare*), abrupt (*it suddenly falls*), but are typical of life as it really is; *sons of men* is a general expression pointing to the commonplaces of life. One's *evil time* might be thought to refer exclusively to the time of death, as Lauha suggests (*cf.* 7:17). But since in other places (*cf.* 8:5–7) the Preacher envisages the flow of events working against all a man's aims and hopes, *evil time* may well refer to other

[1] *Cf.* comment on pp. 69–70.

calamities besides the final one.

ii. Wisdom unrecognized (9:13–16). As elsewhere, the Preacher first relates an observation, then a series of comments and reflections arise from it.

13. The Preacher presents another example of wisdom which he has observed. *I saw* is his regular expression for actual incidents that stirred his reflections; for this reason it should not be treated as a purely fictional parable (*pace* Hengstenberg and others).

14. He was struck by the struggle between prestige (*a great king*) and insignificance (*a little city*); strength (*great siegeworks*)[1] was combating weakness (*few men*). Attempted identifications include Archimedes' saving Syracuse from the Romans by sinking their ships (212 BC), the besieging of Dor by Antiochus the Great (218 BC) and later by Antiochus VII (138 BC), the besieging of Beth-Sura by Antiochus V,[2] the rescue of Athens by Themistocles, the besieging of Abel of Beth-maacah (2 Sa. 20:15–22) and the deliverance of Thebez (Jdg. 9:50–55).

15. In addition to the above theories, Cox thought the *poor man* might be the Preacher himself. None of these is convincing; the point is *no one remembered that poor man*. Does that mean he was forgotten after he had delivered the city? If so, 'we should learn not to count on anything as fleeting as public gratitude' (Kidner). Or was he overlooked when he could have delivered the city? That is more likely, following GNB, NEB and NASV mg.; *he might have delivered the city* (so also Aalders, McNeile, Hertzberg);[3] that is how the succeeding verses apply the lessons of the incident.

16. He applies the lesson of the parable: wisdom is often not heeded. Though wisdom may deliver from the most adverse situations, the humble circumstances of the underprivileged[4] will tell against him and outweigh his wisdom. *Strength* refers to physical prowess, individual or military, and was often noted among royal achievements, as a series of allusions to Israel's

[1] The Hebrew *mᵉsôḏîm* ('nets') is perhaps a slip for *mᵉsôrîm* ('siegeworks') made by copyists. Others (*e.g.* Gordis) argue that *mᵉsôḏîm* itself means 'siegeworks'.

[2] The incidents mentioned are found in Polybius v; Josephus, *Antiquities* xiii; 1 Macc. 6 and 2 Macc. 13.

[3] *Cf.* GK 106(p) for the use of the perfect tense 'to express actions and facts…not as actual but only as possible'.

[4] *Cf.* Ec. 4:13 and footnote 3 on p.95.

archives make clear.[1]

iii. Wisdom thwarted (9:17 – 10:1). 17.

The Preacher continues to emphasize the ease with which wisdom is counteracted. The converse of v. 16 is true, that rulers are able to make themselves heard and wisdom is apt to be lost amidst the clamour. The threefold contrast (*words... shouting, wise... ruler, in quietness... among fools*) brings the point home. A *ruler* is not exclusively the king but anyone from the ruling classes (*cf.* 2 Ch. 23:20; Pr. 22:7). By balancing *wise men* against *ruler*, the author indicates that authority is not necessarily on the side of wisdom. *Shouting* seems to refer here to the shrill self-assurance of a local 'district governor'. The flattering, vociferous company he keeps has a poor influence. There is more hope of wisdom in *quietness* (linked with trustfulness in Is. 30:15 and with contentment in Ec. 4:6). Thus wisdom will not always win its way; clamour, verbosity and power may triumph against it. Wisdom has no built-in guarantees.[2]

18. Another danger is that wisdom is easily overthrown. Some have maintained (*e.g.* Ginsburg) that the erring here is intellectual and that *sinner* has at this point no moral overtones. Yet 'wisdom' and 'folly' are categories with moral overtones in Israel's wisdom literature and in Ecclesiastes in particular. Wisdom involves the characteristically Solomonic largeness of mind, skill in composition, broad knowledge of the natural realm (1 Ki. 4:29–34); but this capacity is divinely given (1 Ki. 4:29), and morally conditioned, since it is given to 'discern between good and evil' (1 Ki. 3:9). In Deuteronomy there are 'statutes and ordinances' to be kept: 'that will be... wisdom' (Dt. 4:5f.). The pattern in Ecclesiastes is essentially the same: largeness of view (1:13), skill in collecting and arranging proverbs (12:9f.), broad interest in the natural realm (1:5–7; 2:4–7), wisdom as divinely given and morally conditioned ('to the man who pleases him', 2:26). In 2:26 'wisdom' is explicitly set over against 'the sinner' in terms that are clearly moral.

---

[1] *Cf.* 1 Ki. 15:23; 16:5, 27; 22:45; 2 Ki. 10:34; 13:8, 12; 14:15, 28; 20:20; 1 Ch. 29:30; Est. 10:2.

[2] The RV takes the verse in a different way: *The words of the wise... are heard more than the cry of him that ruleth.* This depends on how the participle *heard* is attached to surrounding words. Is it 'heard in quietness'? Or '... in quietness is heard'? Since the context is dealing with the limits of wisdom and, therefore, its potential failure (*cf.* verses 11, 16, 18) the RV is less likely. That quiet wisdom is always heard is precisely what is denied by 9:16.

It is doubtful, therefore, whether the moral element can be excluded from the word *sinner* here.

10:1. Despite the chapter division, this verse continues the themes of the previous verses, on a more individual level. The two halves are a comparison and may be translated, '*As dead flies...so a little folly....*' The proverb underlines the fragrance of the wise man's character (*perfumer's oil...wisdom and honour*). Yet only a small mistake makes the smell of his folly greater than the fragrance of his wisdom. Again the proverb warns the readers not to place an ultimate trust even in wisdom. Life must be taken day by day from the hands of God. There is security nowhere else, not even in wisdom.[1]

Folly (*sekel*) or a fool (*sākāl*) is associated with wickedness (7:17) and is the opposite of wisdom (2:19). It results from an inner deficiency of the personality (v.2) which becomes obvious to observers (v.3), especially in the fool's speech (v.14). Elsewhere the foolish are said to be 'skilled in doing evil' (Je. 4:22) and to be characterized by moral insensitivity (*cf.* Je. 5:21). It is a moral rather than an intellectual complaint.

iv. Folly (10:2–3). The rest of the section (10:2–20) considers folly, describing it first in general terms.

2. Folly is traced to a fault in the *heart*, the invisible inner side of man's life contrasted with the face (7:3), hands (7:26) and body (11:10), parts of our outer visible being (*cf.* 1 Sa. 16:7). It includes the mind, for 'to give the heart' to something is to study it (1:13, 17; 8:9, 16). The nature of the *heart* produces the problems the Preacher wrestles with. On the one hand 'eternity' is set within it; we cannot be content with the limitations of the world (3:11); yet it is an evil (8:11; 9:3) and defective heart (10:2). However, God may so deal with us that the heart is occupied with joy (5:20); the heart may be 'put right' (7:3); it may be 'wise' (8:5). The 'dubious anatomy' (Kidner) is deliberate and humorous, as is often the case in wisdom literature. AV and RV translate accurately *A wise man's heart is at his right hand...* The right hand was associated with a strength which saves, supports and protects (Ps. 16:8; Is. 41:13). The right-handedness

---

[1] The Heb. may be translated 'dead flies' or 'deadly flies'. Analogy of usage (*cf.* Heb. of 1 Sa. 5:11; Pss. 7:13; 18:5; Pr. 14:27) points to the latter and is adopted by Leupold. Yet the proverb is much better taken as stressing the smallness of the putrefying influence rather than its deadliness. The analogy of usage is not sufficient to outweigh what is required by the thrust of the argument.

of the Israelite no doubt led him to associate left-handedness with disfavour (*cf.* Mt. 25:33, 41) and fumbling incompetence (*cf.* Jdg. 3:15; 20:16).[1] To have one's heart in the right place is to be skilful and resourceful in one's daily life. To have one's *heart at his left* side is to have the 'springs of life' (Pr. 4:23) located in the realm of practical and spiritual incompetence.

3. The point is made more explicitly. *The fool* loves rowdy songs (7:5) and noisy, shallow laughter (7:6); he is lazy (4:5), garrulous (5:3; 10:12), irascible (7:9), unreceptive to advice (9:17), morally blind (2:14), with a fatal malady at heart (10:2) and disapproved by God (5:4). He may be found in any section of society, even in the temple (5:1) or on a throne (4:13). S. A. Mandry explores the fool's talent for lying, slander, loquacity and infuriating others; he is clever, deceitful, yet supremely confident; he dismisses punishment and any attempts to discipline him; he rebels against religion.[2]

The first part may be translated *he lacks heart* (rsv *he lacks sense*; *cf.* Pr. 10:21) or, construing it differently, 'his heart is lacking'. In view of his inner deficiency (v.2), the latter is likely. The second part has been taken to mean that the fool 'calls everyone who differs from him a fool when they try to correct him…The fool relies on his own judgment and scorns advice' (Jones). This is plausible, seeing that neither gentle persuasion (Pr. 23:9)) nor strong rebuke (Pr. 17:10) affects him. Yet there is nothing about advice in the text; it is better to take it that the fool cannot conceal himself. Thus the fool's inner deficiency comes out in the open for all to see.

v. Folly in high places (10:4–7). **4.** In this whole section on wisdom and folly only this verse and 10:20 contain any note of command. Here the command is followed by the reasons that make it necessary. The *anger*[3] of a *ruler* must be soothed with a calm forbearance that neither panics in fear nor deserts in bitterness. The same vocabulary ('anger…soothed') occurs in Judges 8:3 which illustrates the point.

---

[1] *Cf.* also Z. W. Falk, 'Gestures Expressing Affirmation', *JSS*, 4, 1959, pp. 268f.

[2] S. A. Mandry, *There is No God: A Study of the Fool in the Old Testament* (1972), esp. p. 55; T. Donald, 'The Semantic Field of "Folly" in Proverbs, Job, Psalms, and Ecclesiastes', *VT*, 13, 1963, pp. 285–292.

[3] The Heb. is *rûᵃḥ* ('spirit') but the reference is to anger as in Is. 25:4 ('the anger of the ruthless') and Pr. 29:11.

5. The passage turns to observable (*I have seen*) evils behind the warning of v.4. Some versions soften the statement (NIV *sort of*; RSV *as it were*), but the Hebrew is more likely asseverative ('truly', 'really') than comparative ('like', 'as it were').[1] Leupold holds that the *ruler* is God, arguing that (i) the context makes this plausible; (ii) the Hebrew word (*šallît*) is different from that in v.4 (*môšēl*) and indicates two kinds of ruler; (iii) the definite article in Hebrew points in the same direction; (iv) *šallît* is used of God in Daniel 4:17, 25, 32; 5:21. To which it may be replied: (i) the change of word is merely stylistic variation; (ii) the usage in Daniel is not significant; if *melek* ('king') may be used of both earthly (Is. 6:1) and heavenly (Is. 6:5) kingship, *šallît* may vary in usage similarly; (iii) the article refers to the one ruler on the throne at any one time; (iv) the determining factor is the context, which does not support Leupold's contention. It is concerned with folly in national leadership. It is also unlikely that the Preacher would speak of 'something like an oversight' proceeding from God.

6. 'Time and chance' (9:11) may produce curious reverses, and so limit the effectiveness of wisdom. Men with resources (*the rich*) may lack opportunity; men with opportunity (*high positions*) may lack at least the spiritual resources.

7. In illustration, the Preacher presents an anomaly which would have been more vivid in the ancient world, where *horses* were associated with kingship and wealth (*cf.* Dt. 17:16).

vi. Folly in action (10:8–11). This group of proverbs expounds the consequences of folly. It is difficult to determine the connection with vv.4–7. Possibly the folly which 'proceeds from the ruler' is still in view, but the application appears more general.

8. Vindictiveness has its own built-in penalties. The imagery is similar in Jeremiah 18:18–22. The malicious endeavours of men, often wilful and requiring much trouble (*digs a pit…breaks through a wall*), have a rebound which may be apposite (*He…falls in*), unexpected (8b), and deadly (bitten by a snake). Thus was Haman hanged on his own gallows (Est. 7:9f.)

9. It may be thought that more constructive activities such as quarrying stones and chopping logs are safer than the malicious activities of v.8. Two more proverbs warn against the false

---

[1] *Cf.* comment on 7:7 and Gordis's article on asseverative kaph cited on page 110, footnote 2.

assumption: all life has its inherent dangers.

10. Elsewhere the Preacher and the wisdom tradition in general characterize folly by its superficiality and haste. Here the painstaking aspect of wisdom is presented: a wise man prepares his tools. Thoughtfulness brings success more than brute force.

11. Here the opposite danger is envisaged: one who is able to handle a difficult matter (*a charmer*) fails for lack of promptitude (*the serpent bites...before charmed*). Slackness may nullify inherent skill.

vii. The fool's talk (10:12–14).

12. All wisdom writings deal with the tongue sooner or later, for the character of one's talk is the acid test of wisdom, the 'small rudder' that steers the ship (Jas. 3:4f.). *Wise* words are said to be *gracious*; the Hebrew says they are 'grace', embodying all that is gracious or kindly (*cf*. Ps. 45:2; Pr. 22:11 where the same word is used): appropriate (Pr. 15:23; 25:11), helpful (Eph. 4:29; Col. 3:8), likeable (Pr. 25:12, 15). *Words* may *devour* (literally 'swallow up', *cf*. (Ps. 52:4). They consume the fool's reputation (v.3), his character (Jas. 3:6), his impact for good (Eph. 4:29), and finally the man himself (Mt. 12:36f.).

13. The source of the foolish talk is traced to the inner character (*cf*. Mt. 12:34), the *folly* that has been expounded earlier (*cf*. 10:2f. and the whole of 9:17 – 10:20). Its *end* (outcome; *cf*. 7:8) is *wicked madness* (RSV, NIV), an irrationality which is morally perverse.

14. The Preacher now points to the arrogance of the fool's speech. His verbosity is not founded on any esoteric wisdom or knowledge. He has no knowledge of the present, let alone the future. Nor can any man give him any knowledge of the future. Yet he speaks with conviction on such things.

viii. The fool's incompetence (10:15).

The subject-matter passes from speech to deeds. It has links with vv.16–20, but is not yet looking at the matter on a national level. Any form of *toil* the *fool* finds wearisome. The result is incompetence. The second half of the verse specifies his 'utter ignorance of the things easily come-at-able and familiar to everybody' (Ginsburg). Sloth has already (4:5) been set down as his chief characteristic. Here it is again, a moral and intellectual laziness which leads to a stumbling (2:14), fumbling (10:2), crumbling (10:18) life.

ix. Folly in national life (10:16–20). The whole section reaches a rhetorical climax. Already the Preacher has viewed wisdom and folly in their bearing upon the nation as a whole (10:4–7). Now the cruciality of the issue is pleaded as he weighs up the two ways through life which point to two national destinies: the way of disaster (*Woe...*, v.16) and the way of safety (*Blessed...*, v.17).

16. A nation's first need is a mature leader. RSV *is a child* refers not to age but to general maturity. The term often means 'servant' (*cf.* NIV; but 'is' is possible as well as 'was'; *cf.* also Jdg. 7:10f.; 19:3, *etc.*). In 1 Kings 3:7 Solomon considers himself 'a child' and recognizes his immaturity as a disadvantage to be remedied only by God-given wisdom.

17. The *son of free men* is one whose position in society enables him to act with an independent spirit. The contrast, therefore, is not so much between young and old as between a mature, bold approach to life and an immature, servile manner. Another criterion of national wisdom is self-control. Drinking in the early hours of the day marked a dissolute, slothful approach to life, with emphasis on luxury and personal indulgence. As we have frequently seen (*e.g.* 9:7–10) personal enjoyment had a place for the Preacher; and the antithesis to indulgence here is not asceticism, but self-control. The mark of such pleasure is that it is to be enjoyed 'in a state of strength', not 'in a state of drunkenness'.[1] The enjoyment of life's pleasures as the out-working of a position of wisdom-strength is a mark of national bliss; the pseudo-enjoyment of self-centred indulgence is a mark of national danger.

18. It is not necessary to follow Hertzberg in regarding the *house* as a figure of the nation, thus maintaining the continuity of the passage. The continuity is less intricate, pursuing the theme of folly in the individual citizen. The sluggishness of the fool results not in flashes of divine judgment, but in the more subtle judgment of steady decay. If attention is not paid to the everyday details of life, the results become a crippling liability. RSV, NIV *leaks* may mean 'collapses', the meaning of the cognate Ugaritic verb, and suitable here and in Psalm 119:28.[2] Since, however,

---

[1] The preposition may indicate 'concomitant conditions' (BDB, p. 89), and thus be translated as above.

[2] Suggested by G. Driver in *Archiv Orientalni*, 17, 1949, pp. 155f., and accepted by H. L. Ginsberg, *JAOS*, 70, 1950, pp. 158f.; M. Dahood (CPIQ, 1952, p. 212) and others.

the idea of dripping water is incontestable in Proverbs 19:13; 27:15 and Job 16:20, *leaks* is not an impossible translation.

19. It is difficult to decide how to take this verse. If there is a parallelism in vv.16–19, the antithesis between vv.16f. is repeated in vv.18f., yielding a sequence: woe…bliss…woe… bliss; v.18 is then concerned with the woeful results of the foolish life, v.19 with the happy results of the wise life. Elsewhere *bread* (RSV) stands for the rightful pleasures of life (9:7). That money is said to be *the answer to everything* need not surprise us; despite the Bible's warnings (Dt. 8:13f.; Mk. 10:23ff.; 1 Tim. 6:10), money is never despised. The four references to it in Ecclesiastes reveal one who knew what it was to be wealthy (2:8), that money did not entirely satisfy (5:10), yet found it to be a protection (7:12) and (if we take the passage this way) a practical necessity. Some dispute this view and maintain that the licentious life is still the subject. On this reading the verse describes the limitations of the foolish outlook; it is circumscribed by feasting, wine and money.

The choice is difficult. The present writer considers the latter more likely. The emphases of the Hebrew word-order seem to point this way: 'For *frivolity* they make bread, and it is *wine* that rejoices the living, and it is *money* that is the answer to everything.' The failure of the slothful life is seen here: bread…wine…money is the limit of its horizon.

20. The section closes with a practical word of advice. Neither the king nor the leadership of a nation *(the rich)* must give rise to foolish anger in the wise man's life. The verse challenges us to remain calm in days of national sloth, immaturity and indulgence, and calls for a submissive approach to authority, giving an expedient reason for obedience. The word translated *thoughts* has been rendered 'repose' or 'bedroom', but the common translation is perfectly justified.[1] 'A little bird told me' is a proverb which appears in a variety of forms and cultures, including Aristophanes' *The Birds* and the Hittite *Tale of Elkuhirsa*.[2]

Everything that has been said about wisdom and folly points again to the main lesson of Ecclesiastes: the need to face life as it really is, and take our life day by day from the hand of a sovereign God.

[1] *Cf.* D. W. Thomas, 'A Note on Bᶜmadd'ᵃka in Eccles. 10:20', *JTS*, 50, 1949, p. 177, where a number of other suggestions are mentioned.
[2] *Cf.* T. H. Gaster, 'The telltale bird', in *Myth, Legend, and Custom in the Old Testament* (1969), p. 838.

III. The call to decision (11:1 – 12:8)

Already the book of Ecclesiastes has had an element of exhortation, for the life of faith has been not merely described but commended. The life of indifference and unbelief has been placed against it on the scales and been found wanting. Now the Preacher calls for a verdict.

Often the proverbs of ch. 11 have been treated by expositors as merely a series of shrewd maxims concerning everyday life, dealing only with commerce or sensible agricultural methods (1, 4, 6). It is necessary, however, to understand the over-all thrust as going beyond that, for the Preacher is concerned not merely with details, but with life as a whole. The following factors support this approach.

First, the section is bound together by sustained exhortation, indicating that the whole section is concerned with decisive obedience.

Second, the note of command comes to an impressive and sustained climax in 12:1–7. It is noteworthy that this passage constitutes a single sentence in English translation. The repeated 'before...before...before' (1, 2, 6) rivets our mind to the initial command, 'Remember your Creator'.

Third, the whole section highlights the nature of commitment to Israelite theism. Through a series of minor appeals in ch. 11 flows the theme of faith in the Creator God who is in control of men and their affairs. These epigrammatic commands add up to a grand total underlined in 12:1–8. The whole section is a sustained call to decision, presented in such a way as to call attention to the nature of that decision. We must respond to God without delay, in whole-hearted faith, whether life is adverse or comfortable, for we are marching towards the day of our death.

The Preacher uses homely images in emphasizing the urgency of his message. Modern thinkers might prefer at times to use abstract terms, and we must not miss the Preacher's point in our enjoyment of his picturesque style. For the whole section, coming at this particular point in the book and achieving an elegiac climax of rare beauty in 12:1–7, calls with great urgency for faith in the Preacher's God, the God of Israel.

A. THE VENTURE OF FAITH (11:1–6)

1. The first proverb crystallizes the essence of the Preacher's appeal: it is a call to a venture of faith. The allusion is to the element of trust in much ancient business. Ships on commercial voyages might be long delayed before any profit resulted. Yet one's goods had to be committed to them. Solomon's fleet which brought back 'gold, silver, ivory, apes, and peacocks' (1 Ki. 10:22) sailed once in three years. Similarly the Preacher has called his readers to take life as from the hand of God, and to enjoy it despite its trials and perplexities. Such a life contains within it the elements of trust and adventure (*Cast*), demands total commitment (for *your bread* is used in the sense of 'goods', livelihood', as in Dt. 8:3; Pr. 31:14), and has a forward look to it (*you will find*), a reward which requires patience (*after many days*).

Other interpretations include that of Leupold who sees here a commendation of philanthropy. This has in its favour a parallel in the *Instructions of 'Onchsheshonqy*: 'Do a good deed and throw it into the river; when this dries up you shall find it.'[1] However, the parallel is not exact. The Hebrew reads *bread* rather than 'good deeds'. The point, therefore, is not to urge shrewd foresight in calculated philanthrophy, but shrewd insight in business. The parallel which Leupold cites (Pr. 31:14) likewise points more to the realm of commerce than philanthropy. Other expositors (*e.g.* Jones) find here a reference to commerce, but no more than that. For reasons already given, however, the Preacher probably has in mind the wider subject of obedience to his God.

2. A further aspect of committal is enthusiasm, the dedication of the man of commerce. His investments are to be as widespread as his prosperity will allow. Having commended his over-all world-view, that of Israelite theism, the Preacher is now concerned that the wise man will invest everything he has in the life of faith. The call for urgency is reinforced by an appeal to the unreliability of life. We do not know what calamity may take place *on earth*. Thus the trader is to be zealous about his business, because the unpredictability of events may prevent his zeal in the future.

The numerical sequence *x ... x + 1* (*to seven, or even to eight*)

---

[1] *Cf.* B. Gemser, 'The Instructions of Onchsheshonqy and Biblical Wisdom Literature', *Congress Volume, VTS*, 5, 1960, p. 126.

often expresses an indefinite number.[1] On other occasions, however, the higher number is to be understood literally.[2] Roth considers that in this passage the sequence refers to a 'somewhat indefinite numerical value'. It is more likely, however, that it urges the vigour and full measure of enthusiasm which is required, just as the sequence in Amos 1:3 – 2:6 'probably signified that the measure of guiltiness is more than full'.[3]

Another interpretation sees a reference not to commerce but to philanthropy. Wardlaw contended that the expression *Give a portion* derived from 'the custom of masters of feasts sending portions from before them to the different guests at table' (*cf.* Gn. 43:34), 'or from the practice, on festive occasions, of distributing gratuitously to the poor' (*cf.* Ne. 8:10). If this is so, the essential point is not affected.

3. Some understand the point of this verse to be: God's plan is relentless, therefore carry on regardless (Rylaarsdam). Others: Imitate the generosity of the clouds; your destiny cannot be changed after death (Luther). Others: One cannot control nature, so be prepared for the worst (Delitzsch).

It is closely linked to v.4 by reference to farming. Gordis points out that the two form a chiasmus: rain – wind – wind – rain. The first picture is a storm with heavy rain and violent wind. The second seems to be an uprooted tree. The point is not that the tree could not be moved, but that its fall could not have been anticipated. In this respect RSV and NEB are slightly misleading; better is RV *there shall it be*. The sudden fall of the tree thus contrasts with the gathering storm-clouds, which can be watched with apprehension. The two points involved, therefore, seem to be: Mankind cannot control the difficulties of life, (i) even when he anticipates them, and (ii) because often there are totally unexpected events. These points are made in terms of the farmer's problems, but the over-all unity of 11:1 – 12:8 gives them wider application.

Leupold treats the clouds as a symbol of calamity, and accordingly links this with the latter part of v.2. He also suggests

[1] *Cf.* W. M. W. Roth, 'The Numerical Sequence x, x + 1, in the Old Testament, *VT*, 12, 1962, pp. 300ff.
[2] *Cf.* GK 134(x); G. Wildeboer, *Die Sprüche* (1897), p. 19; C. H. Toy, *A Critical and Exegetical Commentary on the Book of Proverbs* (1899), pp. 127ff.
[3] J. A. Motyer, *NBCR*, p. 730.

that the *tree* may well be 'Israel's proud oppressor Persia'. It is dubious exegesis, however, to turn proverbial imagery into allegory. The only passage in Ecclesiastes to approach allegory is 12:1–7, which contains explicit pointers to its meaning and form. Leupold, however, finds allegory in the 'poor wise man' (9:15f.), the 'prince' (10:7), and sees Persia behind such terms as 'the swift', 'the strong', 'servants', 'fool' (9:11; 10:7, 14), though the Preacher makes no explicit mention of the Persian empire. His reflections concern the problem of human life in general, in every age of history.

4. The Preacher warns next against procrastination, still using an agricultural illustration: faced with erratic wind and weather, the farmer is not to wait interminably for a more propitious occasion to sow his seed. 'Lack of complete knowledge is no excuse for inactivity' (Jones). The life of joy will not come to the waverer. His life will be a total failure. (*Plant...reap* indicates totality.)

5. Interpretations include: (i) 'As you do not know what is the way of the wind, or how bones grow in the womb...' (followed by RV, NIV); (ii) 'As you do not know what is the way of the spirit, or how bones grow in the womb...' (followed by AV); (iii) 'As you do not know what is the way of the spirit in the bones in the womb...'; (iv) 'As you do not know how the spirit comes to the bones in the womb...' (RSV).

The first takes the Hebrew *rûaḥ* to mean 'wind', since it is used in that way in the previous verse and no indication is given of a change in meaning. Hertzberg, who adopts this interpretation, cites John 3:8 as Jesus' allusion to this verse. The second takes *rûaḥ* as the human life or spirit. This gives the verse a certain unity and fits well with the thought of the growth of the human foetus. The third and fourth require the emendation of *ka'ᵃṣāmîm* to *ba'ᵃṣāmîm*. Gordis, who favours this interpretation, argues that if two comparisions were being made the copula ('and', Heb. *wāw*) would be required for *ka'ᵃṣamîm*. This is not necessarily the case, however, for parallel comparisons without *wāw* are attested in the Old Testament (*e.g.* Song 1:5).

It is not possible to be dogmatic in deciding between the first two interpretations. The second, however, is more likely. The mystery of the origin of the human spirit and mysterious growth of the human foetus are two examples of manifest human ignorance. This interpretation demands that the sense of *rûaḥ* change from the previous verse, a possible transition, for *rûaḥ* has already been used in this sense in ch. 3.[1]

Thus at this point in his closing appeal the Preacher simply insists on a fact: certain aspects of God's working on earth defy explanation. The mystery which shrouds our very origin underlies the whole of reality (*cf.* Is. 44:24ff.). In its context this verse drives the reader to a sense of need and warns against an unwarranted optimism in life. The life of faith does not remove the problem of our ignorance; rather, it enables us to live with it. Faith flourishes *in the* mystery of providence; it does not abolish it.

6. The Preacher draws his conclusion. If we are never sure which endeavours will prove fruitful, the right approach to life is to give ourselves to the responsibilities at hand, and await the course of events. The life of faith which leads to joy and contentment does not give infallible knowledge of the future. The Preacher has a doctrine of providence, but it is not a 'calm and tensionless constant'.[2] Negatively the Preacher has forestalled alarm by warning of our ignorance and difficulties; now positively he encourages unremitting diligence.

Some commentators have taken *Sow your seed* to refer to the begetting of children (*e.g.* Graetz), following the Talmud and Midrash, but this is hardly suitable to the context. It is disputed whether *morning...evening* should be taken literally or figuratively. Some treat them as literal 'times of the day' (Jones and others). Others believe that 'Possibly morning and evening are to be taken figuratively, *i.e.* from youth to old age' (Power). The whole verse is an illustration from farming, but beyond that reference there is no further indication that morning and evening have a special figurative sense. The prepositions, best translated '*in* the morning...*until* the evening', simply refer to a good day's work (*cf.* Ps. 104:23); the reference is not to two periods of sowing (*pace* RV). At the same time 'from morning...to evening' is an idiom of completeness (*cf.* comments on 3:1–8).[3] Ginsburg accordingly speaks of the 'two ends of the day denoting the *whole of it, constantly,* vide iii.11; x.13'.

Slack or feeble hands are a biblical picture of inactivity. In the present context 'Do not let down your hand' (literally) warns against discouragement (*cf.* Ecclus. 25:23, where the note of

[1] This view was expounded by Wardlaw, vol. 2, pp. 246–249.
[2] G. C. Berkouwer, *The Providence of God* (1952), pp. 15f.
[3] *Cf.* further, C. H. Gordon, *The World of the Old Testament* (1960), p. 35, footnote; A. M. Honeyman, 'Merismus in Biblical Hebrew', *JBL*, 71, 1952, pp. 11–18.

discouragement is strikingly seen). The believer finds motivation in knowing that life is supervised by God ('the work of God', v. 5) even though detailed prior knowledge of God's plan is not available (*You do not know...*).

B. THE LIFE OF JOY (11:7–10)

God intends for us not only a life of faith but also one of joy. Verses 7f. state the fact and 9f. call on us to realize it in practice.

7. The goodness of life is portrayed by *light* which, as elsewhere in the Old Testament, is used to denote 'joy, blessing and life in contrast to sorrow, adversity and death (*cf.* Gn. 1:3f.; Jb. 10:22; 18:5f.)'.[1] It is being joyfully alive (*cf.* Jb. 3:20; Ps. 49:19). 'Since life is not...truly life unless it can be enjoyed, "light" often designates the pleasures of life (*e.g.* Jb. 10:22; 30:26; Ps. 97:11; Is. 45:7; 60:19–20; Amos 5:18, 20).'[2] Similarly, *to see the sun* means not merely 'to live' but 'to live joyfully'. *See* is occasionally used, as has been shown,[3] to stress the note of enjoyment.

Two words describe the joyfulness of life, *sweet* (*māṯôq*) and *good* (*ṭôḇ*). The latter is a general word, as widely used as the English word 'good'; the former, more precise, is used of the sweetness of honey (Jdg. 14:14), the opposite of 'bitter' (Is. 5:20). The twofold description implies that life is not only good in itself but that it is to be savoured with enthusiasm, as one might enjoy honey.

8. Enjoyment of life is to be life-long, the characteristic of *many years*. Two notes of warning are sounded. First, death makes a response to the life of joy an urgent matter, for earthly life cannot be enjoyed in retrospect. The question of life after death is not raised; *earthly* life is the only subject under discussion. The light of *that* life becomes darkness. No more opportunities will be available to live a life of faith. Elsewhere the Preacher speaks of the 'spirit' of man following a different destiny from that of the animals, implying existence after death (*cf.* commentary on 3:21). Others interpret *the days of darkness* as days of calamity and trial during this life (Wardlaw); this is supported by the fact that *vanity* generally refers to the inherent futility of earthly

[1] E. E. Ellis, art. 'Light', *IBD*, p. 904.
[2] O. A. Piper, art. 'Light', *IDB*, 3, pp. 130–132.
[3] *Cf.* Ec. 1:16 and comments there.

existence (*cf.* 1:4), and that in 5:17 darkness is associated with vexation, sickness and anger during present earthly life. On the other hand 6:4 speaks of death as 'going into darkness' and the entire context of 11:1 – 12:8 clearly urges enjoyment of this life before death overtakes it.

The second warning concerns the inherent *vanity* of life. Life does not yield up its joys easily. *All that lies ahead* in the earthly realm is fundamentally unreliable. For this reason passivity cannot lead to a life of joy. The preceding verses have elucidated the meaning of the vanity of life: it involves delay (1), uncertainty (2), perplexity and difficulty (3f.), ignorance and disappointment (5f.). It is this that makes effort on the part of man so necessary.

9. The call to joy is expounded and pressed in greater detail in 11:9 – 12:8. The *young man* is called to a quest for true joy. The linking *and* (and let your heart cheer…and walk…and know… and remove…and put away…and remember) reminds us that vv.9f. and the ensuing elegy must be taken as a mutually interpreting whole.

The use of *in* (Heb. *b*) is temporal: life in all of its aspects is to be enjoyed *in the time of youth*. Joy is to characterize inner life (*heart*) and outward deportment (*walk*, when used of one's manner of life, generally has reference to its outward bearing).[1] The source and means of joy is the *heart*, the centre of man's whole inner life, the source of thought, feeling, resolution and character. 'Cheerfulness, here, is not merely permitted; it is commanded, and represented as an essential element of piety' (Hengstenberg).

The *eyes* are the instrument of the heart (*cf.* Jb. 31:7); several passages of Scripture link the two (*e.g.* Dt. 28:67; Je. 22:17). The Old Testament speaks of visual beauty (Gn. 2:9, *etc.*) and teaches that the use of sight may lead to joy (Ex. 4:14), wisdom (Pr. 24:32), delight (Song 6:5), or conversely to lust (2 Sa. 11:2ff.), covetousness (Jos. 7:21) and disdain (2 Sa. 6:22).

Joy is to be controlled by the knowledge of God's *judgment*. Leupold is probably right to argue that the definite article ('*the* judgment') points to a single specific event, not merely to God's general judicial activity. It is true that 'the judgment' is used elsewhere in the latter sense (*e.g.* 3:16, Heb.), but here the context points to a definite event. Judgment (*mišpāṭ*) implies *justice:* 'There is a strong flavour of "right" about the word. It does not denote power naked and unashamed, but power dir-

---

[1] *Cf. UBD*, art. 'Walk'; BDB, pp. 234f.

ected towards right ends…. The "judge" is more than simply a ruler. He is one whose activity is fittingly described in terms of law and justice.'[1] It also implies *discrimination*: to judge is to 'discern between good and evil' (1 Ki. 3:9) and with its legal background it frequently carries the notion of deciding between different parties (Gn. 16:5) or of the LORD judging his people (Is. 1:27).[2] The background to the word lies not only in the lawsuit, however, but also in kingship: 'To do justice is part of the royal office'[3] (*cf.* 1 Sa. 8:5), and so it emphasizes God's sovereignty and *power*. Similarly, it is something *dynamic*, for in the face of sin the LORD must take action. His judicial activity is not 'the type of the blindfold maiden holding a balance in her hand'[4] nor 'the cold neutrality of an impartial judge';[5] it is rather the consuming energy in which God must bring about 'right', and thus goes beyond the mere exercise of discrimination to the judicial establishment of kingly rule.

Know here is far more than intellectual perception; it is that grasp of truth which corrects and moulds the life. It 'has an element of acknowledgement. But it also has an element of emotion, or better, of movement of will'.[6] The Preacher's use of a command, not merely a statement, implies that there is a danger of indifference to or neglect of God's kingship and judicial activity.

10. The negative aspect follows. Certain problems which beset 'heart' and 'flesh' constitute hindrances to the life of joy.

The first is *vexation*. The Hebrew *ka'as* refers to that which angers, grieves or irritates. Used elsewhere of the sin of man which 'vexes' God (Dt. 32:19), or the 'provocation' of a woman by a jealous rival (1 Sa. 1:6), in Ecclesiastes it refers to the perplexity (1:18), grief (2:23; 7:3) or irritation (7:9) caused by sheer experience of life. The 'vanity' of the world easily induces in us 'vexation', which hinders the joyful life of faith. The danger is that 'vexation' over the enigmas and irritations of life will grip the 'heart' and that disillusionment will lead to cynicism. Thus the negative counterpart to *rejoice* (v.9) is *remove vexation from your heart*. It makes its resting-place in the inner personality of the foolish (7:9). If we are to live a life of joy, we

---

[1] L. Morris, *The Biblical Doctrine of Judgment* (1960), p. 10.
[2] *Cf.* E. Jacob, *Theology of the Old Testament* (1958), p. 97.
[3] V. Herntrich, *TDNT*, 3, p. 924; *cf.* also H. W. Hertzberg, 'Die Entwicklung des Begriffes *mišpaṭ* im AT', *ZAW*, 40, 1923, pp. 256–287.
[4] E. Jacob, *op. cit.*, p. 99.
[5] Edmund Burke, cited in L. Morris, *op. cit.*, p. 15.
[6] *Cf. TDNT*, I, p. 696.

must learn to cope with cynicism at its root.

The second is that which besets our *flesh*. The Hebrew *bāsār* portrays mankind in his weakness, both physical weariness (12:12) and moral frailty (5:6).[1] This text with its contrast between *heart* and *flesh*, the inner and outer aspects of human life, emphasizes physical weakness. Thus the exhortation is to remove the physical barriers to joy as far as possible. No premium is placed on physical hardships as such. If the removal of bodily pain or discomfort is within reach, it should be taken. The perplexities of life are not solved by asceticism.

E. Jacob understands this verse to refer to gratification of sexual desire,[2] but the passage is not concerned with anything so specific. It operates in general categories.

Attention is often drawn to the contrast between Numbers 15:39 and Ecclesiastes 11:9f. The former is concerned with the danger of disobedience, which is traced to the state of the heart. The latter is concerned with joy, also coming from the heart. Indeed, all aspects of life spring from the heart (Pr. 4:23). Numbers warns against the former;[3] the Preacher encourages the latter.

C. 'TODAY, WHEN YOU HEAR HIS VOICE...' (12:1–8)

The exhortation in 12:1–7 links on to those of ch. 11 ('*And* remember...'), bringing them to a climax. Mankind needs to look not merely to his well-being (11:1ff.) but to his Maker. Expediency and obligation combine. Increasing frailty is portrayed in a series of pictures. The vivid language 'has given rise to the wildest flights of fanciful interpretation' (Hertzberg). No writer has convincingly expounded the passage in terms of a single consistent allegory. Gordis is correct is saying that 'old age is pictured here without one line of thought being maintained throughout'. On the other hand the pictures fall into groups: the two images in v.2 might well be two aspects of an approaching storm, vv.3f. hang together as a picture of a decaying estate.

1. *Creator* is a plural form in Hebrew, suggesting greatness of

---

[1] *Cf.* H. W. Robinson, *The Christian Doctrine of Man* (1913), pp. 24f.; E. Jacob. *op. cit.*, p. 158.

[2] E. Jacob, *op. cit.*, p. 158.

[3] *Cf.* Gordon J. Wenham, *Numbers* (1981), p. 133.

majesty. Some scholars alter *Creator* (*bōr'eḵā*) to 'well' (*bwrk* or *b'rk*),[1] taking the passage to refer figuratively to fidelity in marriage (*cf.* Pr. 5:15–18). Manuscript evidence is lacking. Parallel passages (Dt. 8:18; Ne. 4:14), the gravity of the command (vv.2–6), its religious context (*cf.* 11:9; 12:13f.), all demand the translation 'Creator'.

A further incentive to action is the brevity of life. The days of *youth* are soon past. Increasing age brings inevitable decline, affecting one's whole life. The term *evil* refers not to moral evil but means 'distressing', 'calamitous'. If response is not forthcoming *before the sad days come*, it may never be made. The Preacher has constantly described the life of faith as one of enjoyment (2:24–26; 3:12f., 22; 5:18–20; 9:7–10; 11:8–10). Now he presents another aspect: where God has been neglected, the capacity for joy will be lost. The passing years will press the unheeding reader to self-confessed (*you will say*) despair.

2. It is unnecessary to provide detailed interpretation of *sun...light...moon...stars* (although Delitzsch saw allusion to the spirit, the light of self-examination, the soul and the five senses!). The general idea is clear: the common Old Testament imagery of light and darkness represents the fading capacity for joy. Similarly, the returning clouds refer probably to a continual succession of sorrows. Leupold cites similar imagery in Ezekiel 13:11–13; 38:22. It underlines the inevitability of the problems of old age. 'Even if the storm ceases another one will come soon' (Jones) – a fact easier to appreciate in countries which have a distinct rainy season.[2]

3. The picture now shows particular symptoms of advancing age. The *keepers of the house* suggest the idea of protection and probably refer to the arms. The *strong men* seem to refer to the legs, which elsewhere are linked with strength (Ps. 147:10). The *grinders* are the teeth; *those that look through the windows* are the eyes.

4. It may be that the picture of the great house in decline 'is best taken in its entirety, not laboriously broken down into its constituent metaphors' (Kidner). Certainly there is much diversity of interpretation of the details.[3] If the details are

---

[1] *Cf. JAOS*, 36, 1917, p. 418.
[2] It is possible that the Heb. word for 'after' may at this point mean 'with' (as Scott suggests, and as is the case with the cognate Ugaritic word). *Cf.* also *JTS*, 50, 1949, p. 178.
[3] A brief survey of interpretations of these phrases is provided by Gordis.

significant, the *doors on the street* will refer to the reduced access to the outside world which follows impaired hearing. The next phrase, *when* (RSV; better is Leupold's 'in that') *the sound of the grinding is low*, may extend the image; for the grinding of grain must have been a common cheerful indication that younger folk were going about their business, while the elderly found themselves increasingly shut off from the hum of daily life. Rising *at the voice of a bird* has often been taken to mean that 'the old sleep so lightly that even the twittering of birds will rouse them' (Jones). So much for impaired hearing! More likely the picture is one of waking erratically in the early hours.

Some interpret the reference to *the daughters of song* to participation in singing; some refer to enjoyment of others' singing. There is no need to decide between the two. The Hebrew idiom simply means 'songs', just as 'daughter of Zion' means Zion herself (Mi. 4:10).

5. Imagery is briefly suspended: the old man is fearful of heights and of journeys. The *almond tree* which *blossoms* refers to the hair turning grey, then silver. The *grasshopper* which *drags itself along* refers to the laborious and ungainly walk of the elderly. Or if *the grasshopper is a burden* is the correct translation (RSV mg., less likely), the thought is that the slightest weight becomes burdensome. The next phrase, *desire fails* (RSV), was translated 'the caperberry is made ineffectual' by the LXX (*cf.* RV). No substantiation for this translation has been produced. The caperberry was apparently a stimulant to bodily appetites, so the essential point is unchanged.

The explanation for this decay is now given: man is *en route* to a new home. Various expressions stress different aspects of the climax of decay which is death. First, the Hebrew participle *is going* underlines that 'the going is a continuous act of dissolution which may involve many years in the case of some people' (Leupold). Thus death is the climax of a process which begins in life – a Pauline touch (Rom. 8:10; Phil. 3:21). Second, the transition is irreversible, since it leads to an *eternal home*, a phrase found in the Egyptian *Instructions of 'Onchsheshonqy*.[1] J. Gray wonders whether it might be 'dark house' (on the basis of the cognate root in Ugaritic which can mean 'to be dark'). This is a

---

[1] *Cf.* B. Gemser, 'The Instructions of 'Onchesheshonqy and Biblical Wisdom Literature', *VTS*, 7, 1959, p. 126. D. J. Wiseman informs me it is also a Babylonian/Assyrian idiom for 'grave'.

possibility, but the common Hebrew meaning 'eternity' is preferable.[1] Third, the sadness inevitably linked with the process of dying is stressed: literally, *the wailers go about outside.*

6. The reiterated *before* picks up the thread of v.2 and recalls the main point of this picturesque description. The beauty of the words has a practical purpose: 'Poetry begins in delight and ends in wisdom' (Robert Frost).

The final act of dying is pictured in four expressions, which divide into two pairs. In the first pair a golden bowl is attached to a silver cord or chain. When the chain *is removed* (Hebrew; a variant reading is *is unbound*) the bowl falls and is irreparably damaged. The image points to the value of life (*silver…gold*), and the drama in the end of a life whose pieces cannot be put together again.[2]

The second pair of images visualizes a pitcher lowered into a well by a rope running round a wheel. Death is the smashing of the jar. The terse Hebrew 'The wheel breaks into the well' may be expanded 'The wheel breaks so as to crash down into the well'. The precise wording 'gives us a picture of the ruined apparatus plus the wheel as they have crashed down into the old cistern' (Leupold).[3]

7. The final ignominy is to *return to dust.* Once again (*cf.* 3:20) the Preacher alludes to different aspects of man's nature. *Dust* is what the earth is made of. The word emphasizes mankind's earthly origin (Gn. 2:7; 3:19; Jb. 10:9) and physical weakness (Ps. 103:14). To *return to dust* is to go through the reversal of Genesis 2:7 and to become a corpse, which in turn is liable to further deterioration. It is to be no longer animated by the breath that comes from God (*cf.* Jb. 34:14f.).

The human *spirit* is the principle of intelligent, responsible life.[4] Its withdrawal constitutes the end of earthly life and brings

---

[1] *Legacy of Canaan*, *VTS*, 5, 1965, p. 275.

[2] A golden lamp suspended on a golden chain hung in the Jewish temple at Leontopolis in Egypt in the second century BC, according to Josephus, *Jewish Wars* vii. 10.3. For another interpretation, *cf.* J. E. Bruns, 'The Imagery of Eccles 12:6a', *JBL*, 84, 1965, pp. 428–430. J. L. Kelso (in his study, 'The Ceramic Vocabulary of the Old Testament', *BASOR* Supplementary Studies, Nos. 5–6 (1948), esp. p. 18) says the term *gullah* ('bowl') is used exclusively of metal ware.

[3] M. Dahood (CPIQ, p. 51) takes *galgal* ('wheel') to mean a 'bowl' on the basis of the Akkadian *gulgullu* and the Ugaritic *gl hrs*, 'a golden bowl'. The text would then be translated: 'And the jar is broken at the spring, and the pot is shattered on the well-head'. The Hebrew meaning, however, is well established, and there is no need to see a precise parallel with 'jar'.

[4] See further details on pp. 87–88.

on the dissolution of the body (*cf.* Pss. 22:15; 104:29). Its *return to God* is not developed. It is set, however, in contrast to 'returning to dust', the dissolution of the body, and so cannot refer to that, because it is set in contrast to it. It echoes the contrast of 'upward' and 'downward' in 3:20, and the 'earth' and 'heaven' of 5:2. The term hints, therefore, at continued existence; but we have to wait until the light of the New Testament before details are given (*cf.* 2 Tim. 1:10).

8. Decay and death bring the Preacher back to his opening words. For the phenomenon of death is the supreme example of the earthly realm with which the Preacher began (1:2). Having proved his case, he ends his work.

IV. Epilogue (12:9–14)

The final section[1] gives a brief biographical note on the Preacher (9f.), a commendation (11) and warning (12) concerning wisdom literature, and a final summary of the message of the book (13f.). In some ways it resembles the 'colophon' which the ancient Mesopotamian scribe might add when copying an ancient text. Lauha actually entitles this section 'The Colophon'. Such a colophon might give the catch-line or title of the narrative, a date indicating the time when the scribe was writing, a serial number of the tablet being copied, a statement as to whether the cuneiform tablet did or did not finish the work being transcribed, and the name of the scribe or owner of the tablet.

In the present case v.8 might function as a catch-line in addition to being the climax of chs. 1 – 12. The statement that we have reached *The end of the matter* (v.13) (*cf.* Assyrian *qati* on many cuneiform tablets) may reflect the custom of ancient scribes who, if the work was to be continued on another tablet, might add 'Not finished' to indicate that there was more to be said. Here, says the Preacher, we have a statement that is complete in itself; there will be no major amendments in another chapter. *All has been heard* (13) will be an assurance that what we have in Ecclesiastes is not a misleading series of extracts; it is not 'quickly excerpted' (Assyrian *ḫanṭiš issuḫa*).[2]

9. In his concern for teaching the Preacher was akin to Moses (Dt. 6:1f.), David (2 Sa. 1:18; *cf.* Pss. 34:11; 51:13), Jehoshaphat (2 Ch. 17:7–9), Ezra (Ezr. 7:10), and many other Israelite leaders. He was one of the 'wise men' who taught 'the fear of the LORD'. It is disputable at what time, or whether at all, the *wise* men became a special class, comparable to the prophets, priests and kings. W. H. Gispen warns against bringing West-

[1] For further details concerning the epilogue and its significance in the composition of Ecclesiastes, see Introduction, pp. 40–43.

[2] For further details, *cf.* P. J. Wiseman, *Clues To Creation in Genesis* (ed. D. J. Wiseman, 1977), pp. 143–152; H. Hunger, *Babylonische und assyrische Kolophone* (1968); E. Leichy, 'The Colophon', *Studies Presented To A. Leo Oppenheim* (ed. R. M. Adams, 1968). In a private note D. J. Wiseman comments: 'These correspond with the similar formulae in Babylonian colophons, which indicate the care taken in preserving and presenting the material.'

ern ideas of 'professions' to the subject. D. A. Hubbard distinguishes between the 'officially' wise and the 'simply' wise, and suggests that the Israelite tradition emerged largely from the latter 'without concern for an official ministry of teaching or counselling'.[1] It is not possible to be dogmatic. The contrast with *the people* seems to indicate a recognized position. It is sometimes suggested that the Preacher was a member of a wisdom 'school', but this goes beyond the evidence.

*Besides...also...*suggests that it was possible to be a wise man without 'teaching the people'. The Preacher's concerns were pastoral, not professional. Accordingly the *knowledge* he taught must be understood as more than accumulation of facts. It is closely related to discipline, skill and righteousness (Pr. 1:1-6; 12:1). Its starting-point is the 'fear of the LORD' (Pr. 1:7). Although taught by men such as the Preacher, and acquired by effort (Ec. 2:21), it is nevertheless a gift of God (Pr. 2:6) and morally conditioned: 'to depart from evil is understanding' (Jb. 28:28). Ultimately it is fellowship-knowledge, that comes in the context of knowing a person (Pr. 2:5).

The Preacher's skill at his task is set before us in three verbs: *pondered, searched out, arranged.* The first (literally 'weighed', a rare word) points to careful evaluation, indicating his honesty, caution and balance; the second to thoroughness and diligence. The third, *arranged*, points to the skilful orderliness of his presentation and reminds us that there is an artistic element in his work (as in all preaching and writing).

His medium was *many proverbs.* The 'proverb' (*māšāl*) had a wide range of meaning. It could include such things as Jotham's fable (Jdg. 9:7-15), the riddle of Samson (Jdg. 14:12ff.), the witticisms concerning Saul and David (1 Sa. 10:12; 18:7), the 'proverb of the ancients' (1 Sa. 24:13) and Nathan's parable (2 Sa. 12:1ff.). Its techniques abounded in crisp sayings (1 Ki. 20:11; Je. 23:28; 31:29), parallelisms (Pr. 18:10), comparisons (Pr. 17:1), numerical sequences (Pr. 30:15ff.), acrostic patterns (Ps. 37; Pr. 31:10-31), allegories (Is. 5; Ec. 12:2ff.), aphoristic questions (Am. 6:12) and similar devices, all geared to piercing the crust of indifference.

10. Further characteristics of his ministry are underlined.

---

[1] W. H. Gispen, 'The Wise Men in Israel', *Free University Quarterly*, 5, 1957, p. 2; R. N. Whybray, *The Intellectual Tradition in the Old Testament* (1974), ch. 2; D. A. Hubbard, *TB*, 17, 1966, p. 17, following S. Blank, 'Wisdom', *IDB*, 4, p. 856.

First, he realized that *pleasing words* (lit. 'words of delight') have a penetrating effect that slapdash and ill-considered words lack. Second, his words are written *uprightly*. The two characteristics balance each other. His words are not so *pleasing* that they cease to be *upright*. Attention to form at the expense of content would lose the verdict of his God (v.14; *cf.* 2 Cor. 4:2f.). To be upright but unpleasant is to be a fool; to be pleasant but not upright is to be a charlatan. Third, his message consists of *words of truth*, on which, like other wise men, he sets a high premium (*cf.* Pr. 8:7; 22:21, *etc.*). Fourth, his ministry involved writing as well as speaking. Like law-givers (Ex. 24:4), judges (1 Sa. 10:25), kings (2 Ch. 35:4), prophets and psalmists, the wise man was concerned to perpetuate his teaching in writing.

11. The *goad* (*dorbānâ*) is mentioned in the Old Testament only here and in 1 Samuel 13:21 (*dorbān*). It was probably a large sharp-pointed stake used to prod an animal. The *nail* (*maśmēr*, elsewhere spelt with a different sibilant, *masmēr*) ranged from the large gold nails used in Solomon's temple (2 Ch. 3:9) to the smaller iron nails used for 'doors...and...clamps' (1 Ch. 22:3). The two words speak of the twofold effect of the Preacher's words, which stimulate to action and establish teaching in the memory. The phrase 'masters of assemblies/collections' (Heb.) is probably correctly rendered *collected sayings* (RSV). The Hebrew idiom 'master of x' is used to mean 'a person or thing whose dominant characteristic is x'. The meaning here depends on whether people (assemblies) or things (collections) are in mind. The latter is more likely because of the parallelism: *The sayings of the wise...goads...collected sayings...nails*.

The *Shepherd* has been taken to refer to the king (*cf.* 1 Sa. 25:7) or to God himself (*cf.* Pss. 23:1; 80:1). The latter is more likely, since the name 'Preacher' has already been given to the originator of the material of the book (vv.9f.). Although his words are the result of his own reflections, at the same time they come from God. There is here, therefore, a doctrine of inspiration. The Preacher (or his editor) is conscious of his own activity (v.10) with regard to both the form (v.9) and the content (v.10) of his work; yet he contends that the finished product is the word of God as well as the word of man. There are different kinds of inspiration within Scripture. Some involve a high degree of personal involvement and reflection on the part of the inspired writer; at the other end of the scale is the writer who records a revelation presented by an angelic messenger, which may totally bewilder the recipient. Wisdom-inspiration is undramatic in its mode; the work of the Spirit and the reflection of the writer form an inseparable continuum. Wise men as well as prophets 'moved by the Holy Spirit spoke from God' (2 Pet. 1:21).

12. In the closing remarks a warning is given comparable to those which close a number of biblical writings (*cf.* Rom. 16:17–20; 2 Thes. 3:14f.; 1 Tim. 6:20f.; 1 Jn. 5:21; Rev. 22:18f.). *Beyond these* refers back to the sayings 'given by one Shepherd', outside of which caution is required. The form of words used has a reflexive force: 'take warning', 'admonish yourself'. It points to the private judgment and responsibility of the individual reader.

The *making of many books*[1] began long before any conceivable date for Ecclesiastes. Writing was well established as a hallmark of civilization from about 3500 BC onwards. 'Books' were written first on clay tablets, later on papyrus or leather. When an alphabetic script came into Syria-Israel in the second millennium BC, it brought the possibility of 'no end' of books. A mass of cuneiform tablets, ostraca and papyri exist to prove the point.[2] Evidently there was much in this body of literature that the wise man thought fit to warn against, since it did *not* 'come from one Shepherd'. Israel shared much with the wisdom traditions of surrounding nations and doubtless had profited from its acquaintance with pagan literature (*cf.* Acts 7:22), as did the apostle Paul in a later age (Acts 17:28; Tit. 1:12). Yet the Old Testament also warns that pagan wisdom stands under the ever-imminent judgment of God (*cf.* Is. 19:11ff.; Ezk. 28:2ff.), as does the New Testament (1 Cor. 1:17ff.; 2:6). No doubt within Israel too there could be a 'wisdom' that deserved rebuke rather than discipleship (*cf.* Je. 8:9).

A more pragmatic reason for caution is the physical effect of *much study*. The would-be wise man 'will make his study a prison and his books the warders of a gaol'.[3] The term *flesh* generally points to weakness and here indicates our physical frailty.

---

[1] It has been pointed out to me that if the Heb. pointing is ignored it is possible to translate 'making of many scribes', but the verb ('*āsāh*) never seems to be used of a person in this way. References elsewhere to 'making' a father (Gn. 17:5), a king (2 Ch. 2:11), a slave (1 Ki. 9:22), a prince (1 Ki. 14:7), a prophet (Je. 1:5), a priest (Je. 29:26), a watchman (Ezk. 3:17), all use a different verb, *nāṭan*.

[2] *Cf.* D. J. Wiseman, 'Books in the Ancient Near East and in the Old Testament', *The Cambridge History of the Bible* (ed. P. Ackroyd, 1970), vol. 1, pp. 30–48.

[3] C. H. Spurgeon, *Lectures to My Students*, 1 (1875), p. 172.

13. The Preacher's message is summarized in two points which concern the greatness of God and the Word of God. The Hebrew emphasizes the words *God* and *commands*. The *fear* of God is the realization of his unchanging power and justice (3:14). It delivers from wickedness and self-righteousness (7:18) and leads to a hatred of sin (5:6f.; 8:12f.). If it is the 'beginning of wisdom' (Ps. 111:10; Pr. 1:7; 9:10) it also is *the end*, the conclusion; no progress in the believer's life leaves it behind. Nor is the testimony of the New Testament any different (*cf.* 2 Cor. 7:1).[1]

The reader is urged to *keep his commandments*. The order of the two points (*fear...keep*) is significant. Conduct derives from worship. A knowledge of God leads to obedience; not vice versa. This is the only place in Ecclesiastes where the *commands* of God are mentioned. The body of the book has simply placed two alternative views of life over against each other and the life of faith has been commended. Now in the epilogue, almost as an aside, it is pointed out that such a life will have implications. It must not be restricted to the Mosaic law. It refers to all that is known to be God's will. The last phrase reads literally: 'For this is the whole of the man.' Elsewhere in Ecclesiastes, however, the 'whole of the man' is a Hebrew idiom for 'every man' (*cf.* 3:13; 5:19). The sense, therefore, is 'This applies to everyone'.

14. A final reminder repeats teaching found earlier in the book (3:17; 11:9). A new note is the warning that *every hidden thing* will be brought within the embrace of God's verdict. The 'hidden things' which the law rebuked (Lv. 4:13) and the psalmist confessed (Ps. 90:8) will not escape the assessment of God (*cf.* 1 Cor. 4:5). The Preacher's God combines within himself grace (2:24f.; 3:12f.; 9:7–9) and judgment. The life of faith is offered; the warning of judgment is held out alongside. Let men rejoice (11:9), but let them also remember (12:1) and fear (12:13)!

---

[1] *Cf.* J. Murray, *Principles of Conduct* (1957), ch. 10, 'The Fear of God'.

POSTSCRIPT

In this commentary I have tried to resist the temptation of treating the Preacher as a twentieth-century thinker; and with the exception of the term 'secularism', for which I could find no precise ancient equivalent, I have avoided twentieth-century theological or philosophical terminology. Yet, when 'all has been heard', the message of Ecclesiastes is strikingly relevant to this century. For it is twentieth-century man who is supremely troubled about being 'thrown into existence' and asks why is there something rather than nothing. Probably the twentieth century, at least in the western world, is the most bored epoch the world has yet seen. 'Stop the world, I want to get off' is a popular cliché. Western intellectual tradition from Schopenhauer onwards has been preoccupied with 'life's ultimate certainty', the fact of death. Albert Camus wrote, 'There is but one truly serious philosophical problem and that is suicide.'[1]

Modern man is also a striking confirmation that the universe sours when secularism grips his thinking. He loses his love of nature which becomes caught up in his weariness. 'The sun shone, having no alternative on the nothing new' begins a twentieth-century novel,[2] giving Ecclesiastes 1:3 a further turn of the screw. Similarly, history is no longer seen to have any purpose. The Judeo-Christian tradition with its linear view of history has been replaced either by some kind of determinism in which man, individually or collectively, plays no significant creative role and so has no meaning, or by a cyclical view in which all human achievement returns inevitably to chaos and so is ultimately futile.[3]

This purposelessness is no mere academic stance, but a hideous reality that permeates the consciousness of the whole of

---

[1] A. Camus, *The Myth of Sisyphus* (Penguin Books, 1975), p. 11.
[2] Samuel Beckett, *Murphy* (1938).
[3] See further David Bebbington, *Patterns in History* (1979).

society and gnaws away mercilessly at the human soul. There is no exit. The universe is silent before all questions and mankind knows what Blaise Pascal meant in saying, 'I am terror stricken before the silence of infinite space.'[1] He shuns talk about death as the Victorians shunned talk about sex. Meanwhile the 'man in the street' spends his time shielded by the television screen or by the popular newspapers with ready-packaged thinking and diverting entertainment.

To such a world Ecclesiastes has something to say. He does not come as a formal philosopher; it is a word from God he has to share, despite his reflective low-key approach. He does not present half-a-dozen arguments for the existence of God. Instead he picks up our own questions. Can you cope with life without having any idea where you are going? You don't have all the answers to life's enigmas, do you? Your neo-pagan view of life doesn't give you any hope of achieving very much, does it? Nature will not answer your questions, and you are bored by it anyway. History baffles your attempts to understand it. You don't like to think about your own death; yet it is the most certain fact about your existence.

What would it be like, asks the Preacher, if things were utterly different from what you thought? What if this world is not the ultimate one? What if God exists and is a rewarder of those who seek him? What if one of his supreme characteristics is his utter, incredible generosity, his willingness to give and give and give again, his utter acceptance of us just as we are? Could it be, asks this provocative and seemingly negative Preacher, that the barrenness and hideous purposelessness of life stems only from the fact that you will not believe in such a God?

We leave the Preacher there. His message is not complete, for he lived before the full light of the gospel of Jesus Christ. He saw 'afar off', and still leaves us with some questions. How *can* God accept us in such a way? What is the explanation of the hideous mess of this world? On what grounds can he feel confident that some future judgment will put it all right? Is there not a missing link in all this? The missing link is Jesus Christ the Son of God. It is in Christ, the Saviour and sin-bearer, that God says to us: 'God is reconciled to you...You be reconciled to God' (2 Cor. 5:18ff.). He has set a day when he will judge the world with justice by the man whom he has appointed. He has given proof

---

[1] *Pensées*, no. 392 in the Everyman edition (1960), p. 110.

of this to all men by raising him from the dead (Acts 17:31).

'Some...sneered...Others said, "We want to hear you again." ...A few...believed.'